M000274162

Rusty Wilson's

Canadian Bigfoot Campfire Stories

© 2014 Yellow Cat Publishing™

All rights reserved, including the right of reproduction in whole or in part in any form.

ISBN: 978-0-9849356-9-7

Yellow Cat and the accompanying logo are registered trademarks owned by Yellow Cat Publishing.

www.yellowcatbooks.com

Names, characters, places, and incidents either are the product of the author's imagination or are used fictitiously. Any resemblance to actual persons, living or dead, events, or locales is entirely coincidental.

I suspect that Canada has more wild things than we could imagine in our wildest dreams. If you take a look at a map, you'll see just how immense and rugged many parts of this country are, especially those regions in the north and around the Canadian Rockies and Coastal Mountains. I'm sure there are things out there we could only imagine, one of them being Bigfoot—or Sasquatch, as our northern friends call him.

—Rusty Wilson

· F O R ·

Aleksandra Caledonia

Contents

Foreword

Greetings, Fellow Adventurers!

Even if you're an armchair adventurer, you still qualify as an adventurer, because you have the desire to learn and discover new things.

Some discoveries we can make on our own, but sometimes it's almost as good hearing what others have experienced. This is why I love sitting around a campfire with my fly-fishing clients, listening to them talk about their adventures. I hear about things I would never see on my own.

It's quite a treat, and the intent of my Bigfoot campfire books is to share some of these fun (and sometimes scary, but almost always wild) adventures with you.

And speaking of wild things, I suspect that Canada has more wild things than we could imagine in our wildest dreams. If you take a look at a map, you'll see just how immense and rugged many parts of this country are, especially those regions in the north and around the Canadian Rockies and Coastal Mountains. I'm sure there are things out there we could only imagine, one of them being Bigfoot—or Sasquatch, as our northern friends call him.

Sasquatch legends go back into the misty histories of many native peoples of Canada, making me think that the creatures migrated across the Bering Straits from Asia, as did the ancestors of the native Americans. Maybe they even waved to each other on the trail, for many natives revere the Sasquatch.

The stories in this book come from the Canadian provinces of British Columbia and Alberta, and though I'm sure the Sasquatch Nation thrives in many other parts of Canada, especially the untouched northern reaches, these two provinces are where most of my fishing clients come from, bringing their stories with them. It's logical they would come my way when seeking out guided fishing trips in the U.S., as I'm based in Montana and Colorado, not far from their part of the country.

In addition, my wife Sarah and I took a trip a few years ago up into the Okanagan Valley of British Columbia, where I collected several of these stories from locals, stories I've included.

I'm sure one could fill many books with stories of the Canadian Sasquatch, and perhaps there will be more to come, but for now, pull up a chair or log, kick back with some hot chocolate, and be prepared to hear some tales that will make your hair stand on end—or maybe make you wonder if you might like to meet the Big Guy himself.

—Rusty

1. The Thwarted Adventurer

This is a story told by a fellow from a little town called McBride in British Columbia, not too far from the bigger town of Prince George. When I first met Al, we were fishing in the beautiful area around Craig, Montana.

When I saw his contact address was in Phoenix, I didn't think much about it, but when I heard his distinct Canadian accent, I had to find out more about his roots. Sure enough, he was from B.C., and he had the following interesting story about one of the most stunning places in the world, Kakwa Provencial Park.

—Rusty

My name is Al, and I grew up in the small town of McBride in British Columbia. McBride is in the Robson Valley on the Yellowknife Highway going to the town of Prince George, though it's closer to Mt. Robson Provincial Park, home to B.C.'s second-highest mountain.

McBride owes its existence primarily to logging and farming, though it's slowly becoming more of a tourist town. But it's a small, close-knit town of maybe around 600 people, so everyone knows what everyone else is doing.

My dad ran a restaurant and my mom worked at the community center, so we knew everyone in town (not that it was hard to do). And like I said, they all knew what we were up to, which was a big detriment to a teenaged boy who wanted nothing more than to live a life of freedom and unaccountability.

McBride is in a big valley, with the magnificent Canadian Rockies to the east and the more gentle Cariboo Mountains to the west. As a kid looking out my window, I could always see mountains, and I think this bred a bad case of wanderlust in me, something I still have to this day.

McBride is a great place to live if you love the outdoors—in the winter there's cross-country skiing and snowmobiling, and in the summer there's hiking, camping, mountain biking, and lots of bird watching.

But if you're a teen in McBride, there really isn't that much to do, especially when your parents prohibited you from exploring and camping, unless I was with them. And they were so busy they rarely had time to get out.

Even though I put up lots of good arguments, my parents refused to let me go out into the backcountry, whether alone or with my friends. Maybe it was the fact that this part of Canada is especially wild, but I think it had more to do with the occasional bear stories that would make the rounds. Or more likely, it was because my dad was from the city—Calgary. I think they worried about things too much, especially wild things.

In any case, I was a thwarted adventurer, and it really rankled me at times. I remember sitting in the classroom fantasizing about climbing and exploring the mountains out my window.

One day, when I was about 15, I asked my mom why other kids were allowed to go out camping together but I couldn't. Was she really that afraid I'd get eaten by a grizzly? As far as I knew, nobody around McBride had ever had a serious encounter with a bear.

She just told me it was something more ominous, as if there could be anything more ominous than a big brown bear. She said she and Dad had both heard the stories and there were fewer and fewer McBride parents letting their kids go out alone into the woods.

"What stories?" I asked.

"The stories of a huge hairy wild man that lives up in the mountains, a creature called Sasquatch," my mom replied. "It would be irresponsible of us to let you go out into the very places it's been reported. When you get out of school, you can move to a place that's safe and explore to your heart's content. But not here."

I had heard the stories, too, though I wouldn't admit it to my parents. They always made a chill run up my spine, though I pretty much didn't believe in Sasquatch, especially considering some of the sources of the stories, people I knew who had wild imaginations, like Billy Thomas.

Billy claimed a Sasquatch had come right up to his house window and peered in, and we all knew he had to be lying, just like he'd lied about meeting Queen Elizabeth and her entourage once out in the middle of some Crown forest in Alberta. He was nuts.

Anyway, I was allowed to mess around in the valley with friends, but I couldn't do things I read about, like solo backpacking in Revelstoke and Glacier national parks (and yes, there is a Glacier National Park in Canada, just like in Montana). I wasn't even allowed to go backpacking with friends, yet alone solo.

My dad was a bred and born Canadian, but my mom was from the United States. I have dual citizenship because of her, and I now spend most of my time in the U.S.

My wife and I have a little place near Phoenix, Arizona, where we spend winters. We go back to the family home in McBride each summer, but when my parents are gone someday, I'll sell the house there. We only go back so our kids can spend time with their grandparents.

I have to say that, after all the years of resentment against my parents for keeping me on such a short leash in my youth, I now do the same with my two sons when we're in McBride. In fact, that leash may be even shorter than the one I had, and this story will explain why.

When I was 17, me and some buddies decided to visit Kakwa Provincial Park. There were three of us, and we'd spent lots of time mountain biking around the valley and were in great shape.

We were all near graduation from high school, and we all had plans to leave the valley in the fall, going off to college in various places. I spent the next two years at the College of New Caledonia in Prince George, then transferred to the University of Calgary. I now work in health-care as an administrator.

Imagine, if you can, what it's like to live at the gateway to one of the world's most epic places and never be allowed to go there. This place was Kakwa.

Anyway, we decided we were going into Kakwa, no matter what. I've always been an honest person, so I was straight up with my parents. I told them our plans and ended my argument by saying it was a crying shame I would be leaving McBride soon having never been into Kakwa, and how would I ever explain that deficit in my life to future friends?

My dad had been to Kakwa—he flew into Kakwa Lake once and spent three days fishing, and he knew how beautiful it was, so he could relate.

My mom, on the other hand, had no desire to see her young son eaten by a brown bear or worse, especially since her job of raising him was almost done. She was adamant at saying no, and there was nothing I could do to change her mind.

My other buddies were having the same problem. None of them were making any headway convincing their parents that someone who grows up in McBride is deprived by not seeing Kakwa. We felt it was borderline child abuse.

We got together at the local hangout (not my dad's cafe, as he would watch us too close), and over burgers we decided we had to take drastic action. Maybe we could somehow pool our savings and have a bush pilot fly us in. The park has camp hosts there in the summer, so maybe we could convince our parents to let us fly in for a couple of days if we promised to stay at the lake and fish. We'd forget mountain biking in and hiking, it was too arduous of a trip getting in that way, anyway, over 20 miles on an old road with several river crossings.

OK, we had a new plan. We all went home and were actually able to convince our parents to let us do this. My dad and mom knew the camp hosts who spent the summer in a cabin there. My folks would talk to them next time they came out for supplies, as there's no cell service there, though they did have satellite phones.

We were ecstatic! We were going to fly into Kakwa, which would be much better than toiling our way in on mountain bikes. We could stay three full days, then the bush pilot would come pick us up.

But we were in no way to leave the lake, and the camp hosts would strictly enforce this. No hiking up onto the big massive peaks. We'd have to be content with seeing them by bush plane.

I had only flown a couple of times in my life until then, and that was on big jets out of Prince George to go visit my grandparents in Oregon, so the thought of flying into Kakwa and actually landing on the lake would be an adventure all in itself.

We would then camp at the campground near the host cabin and spend our time pretending to fish, as none of us were avid fisherman. But what that meant was that we could theoretically hike around the lake and still not be breaking any rules. And if you've ever seen photos of Kakwa Lake, you know it's huge and is just as wild as the rest of the park. In fact, in some ways it's wilder, as wildlife needs water and tends to stay near lakes and such, so we might see something interesting (and I did, but not what I expected).

Finally, the day came when our chartered plane was to take us into the depths of one of Canada's most rugged and beautiful areas, and that's saying a lot. Of course, none of us had the money to pay for a chartered plane, but my dad generously threw a few hundred loonies (Canadian dollars) into the pot to make up the difference, telling me it would be my birthday and Christmas gifts together.

He knew I would soon be leaving for college, and I think he knew there wouldn't be many more times he could do something like this for me, as I'd be gone. Little did he know how much college would cost, even though I worked and got a scholarship, but that's another story.

The anticipation and fear I had when we boarded that little STOL Cessna was almost culpable. STOL means "short takeoff or landing," and those little planes can land or takeoff in 30 or 40 feet, sometimes less.

It didn't take long to get from McBride to the lake. Floating across the blue glacial waters of Kakwa Lake in that plane was something I'll never forget. I felt like I was in a dream from the moment the plane's floats skimmed across the water. In fact, I felt like I was in a dream the entire time I was there, the place was so far beyond anything I'd ever seen.

Little did I guess that dream would become a nightmare, one as far beyond description as is Kakwa Provincial Park.

We unloaded our gear and stood in disbelief as we watched the float plane take off, disappearing into the distance, our only connection to civilization. Sure, we were McBride kids, we grew up in what some might consider Canadian backcountry, but in reality, it was nothing compared to this.

We were truly in the wilds and it made us feel a bit unsettled, to be honest, knowing a 1200 pound brown bear might be watching us from behind that big tree over there and there was nothing we could do, nowhere we could run, and we couldn't even jump in the lake, as brown bears are excellent swimmers.

Of course, this frame of mind made us completely unprepared to see all the other people in the campground. We were far from alone, and while we were there, several groups of horse and mule riders came into camp from the Alberta side of the park.

We soon met the camp hosts, Jan and Bill, and they told us the rules: no eating in tents, keep a clean camp, food goes into the bear cans, etc. Nobody wanted any nocturnal bear visits, so everyone seemed to be really careful with food.

Never go out alone, we were told. Always go out in small groups. Our group of three was almost too small, but as long as we carried bear spray and made noise, they said we'd be okay.

"You boys know we've been advised to keep an eye on you. Your parents don't want you to leave the lake. Agreed?" Bill reminded us.

We all nodded our heads, but none of us showed any enthusiasm for the rule.

Bill continued, "Let me tell you, we had two backpackers have a bear encounter last week. Only one made it back. We've had extensive search and rescue activities, and there's been no hide nor hair of the other, a gal missing over by Mount Ida. The one who came out alone said they'd been attacked by what looked to be a giant brownie. It's rare for a brown bear to consider humans as prey, but it's almost fall and they're trying to build up fat reserves for hibernation. So, stay by the lake. The area where the girl is missing is closed."

This sounded pretty serious, and we agreed to stay by the lake, now having a great deal more enthusiasm for the plan.

That night, even though there were others in the camp-ground, we felt the immensity of the natural world and the untouched wilderness we'd been transported into, a place that felt so wild it made me think of what it must've been like to have been an early mountain man.

We sat around our little camp stove, making freeze-dried stew, then followed that with hot tea, the late July chill reminding us where we were and how early winter arrived there.

We talked about the park, then about our lives back home, then about college and how nervous we all felt about leaving home for the first time. Finally, seeming to have run out of things to say, we just sat there in silence.

Eventually, one of my buddies, Mark, said, "I wonder what happened to that woman?"

Lance, my other buddy, asked, "What lemon?" Lance was always either kidding around or telling us how brave he was.

Mark ignored him and answered his own question, "A bear probably got her. Oh man, what are we going to do if a great big grizzly comes into camp, hungry, in the middle of the night?"

"Give him that big hunk of baloney," Lance replied.

"That would be like eating one bite of a burger to a bear," I said. "It would just make him hungrier."

"Then we'll throw Lance to him," Mark said.

This kind of broke the suspense, but we were still look-ing over our shoulders. It was late, and we could see that the other campers had all crawled into their tents. I was envious of the camp hosts over in their little cabin. I knew their satellite phone was our only connection to any kind of outside help, and I admired their courage to come out here and live in the wilds, even in a cabin.

And yet, the rewards were immense. To see the beauty of Kakwa around you all day every day must be the total apex of one's life. I suddenly wanted to live out there with them, but also in a cabin. (I've since heard that a few years ago a new cabin was built for hosts, plus one for campers. How I wish it had been there when we were.)

We sat, silent, when suddenly the hair on the back of my neck stood up. In the far distance, I could hear what sounded like the call of a wolf.

"Dang, there's wolves out here," said Lance nervously.

Mark started laughing. "There probably are wolves out here, you fool, but that's no wolf, it's a loon."

The loon cried again, a distant mournful sound, trying to locate its mate in the darkness. We all sat, transfixed. Soon, we could hear what must be the mate, calling back in the same mournful haunting way.

We were tired and soon climbed into our tents, and even though I figured I wouldn't be able to sleep from thinking about bears, I hardly remember crawling into bed, I was so tired.

I woke in the dark, but my watch said it was past time to get up. The days were getting shorter that far north. Back at home, I barely noticed it was dark outside when I got up, as my parents would already have the lights on and breakfast cooking. Out here, it seemed too early to get up, but my watch said it was 7 a.m.

I tossed and turned a bit, uncomfortable on the hard ground, even though I had a pad. It seemed to be slowly losing air.

I suddenly froze. Something was next to my tent, and I could hear a low guttural growl. Holy crap! What was it? I didn't dare move, holding my breath.

Now I could hear Mark saying, "Shut up, you fool. Go growl somewhere else. Go growl at the moon."

I started laughing and felt relieved, yet just a bit miffed. Crawling from my tent, headlamp on, I flashed the light right in Lance's face, where he crouched next to my tent.

"Ever hear the story about the boy who cried wolf?" I asked.

"Yeah, except it's loon, not wolf," Lance replied.

Mark said, "Hot water's boiling. Tea or coffee?"

"Coffee for me," I replied. "There's freeze-dried eggs and bacon for breakfast, but maybe we should hold off until later. Don't want the smell of food drawing something in until we can see it, at least."

"That bunch in the next site is cooking something that smells like *real* bacon," Lance said.

We sat around and talked and drank coffee as the sun rose and then fell silent at the spectacle of reds and golds and pinks like crowns on the mountain tops. Loons called to one another across the lake.

Finally, as the sun broke over the highest peaks and lit the very tops of the tall trees all around the lake, reflecting in the still waters, we made our breakfast and ate.

"Anybody check the weather report before coming in here?" Mark asked.

I replied, "It's supposed to be nice the whole time."

"What about that saying, red sky at dawn, sailor be warned?" Lance asked.

"I don't think it applies to a few stray clouds," I answered. "What do you guys want to do today?"

Mark said, "Nothing. Just hike around the lake."

"Nothing?" Lance replied. "That's a long hike."

"We don't have to go all the way. If we run out of beach, we'll turn around."

We gathered our daypacks and fishing gear and started off, walking along the beach.

It wasn't long until Lance said, "Geez, look at this! Bear tracks. And here's a log that's been turned over. And bear scat."

"That means *we* should scat," Mark replied. "Let's go the other direction."

We all three turned at once and headed the other way, which took us past the camp hosts' cabin. We told them about the tracks. They didn't seem too concerned—after all, we were in bear country, deep in the heart of British Columbia. Bears came with the territory.

We continued along the lake, periodically checking our bear spray canisters in their handy chest holsters. Yep, still there.

Finally, after an hour or so of trudging along, we stopped for a break. The stunning scenery still felt dreamlike, and I didn't have to ask the others if they felt the same way, as it was written across their faces, plus there was very little of the banter we usually engaged in.

We now stopped and sat on some big rocks by the shore. Normally, we would be skipping rocks and throwing sticks and writing our names in the soft sand, but instead we sat in silence.

Finally, Lance pointed to a slope high above on the flanks of a huge mountain, saying, "It would be so cool to climb up there."

"We can't," I replied. "We promised."

Lance said, "Nobody would know but us."

Mark replied, "Unless we got into trouble. There aren't even any trails out here to speak of. Don't you think it would be spectacularly stupid to just take off without a plan, a compass, a GPS, all that survival stuff, and not even tell anyone?"

"Yeah it would be pretty reckless," said Lance. "But I feel reckless."

I answered, "Go ahead. You may end up missing, though. Like that woman hiker who disappeared. I wonder what happened to her? Bears? Sasquatch?"

"Sasquatch? You think so?" asked Lance with surprise.

"Maybe."

The conversation went on like this for some time, rapidly deteriorating from the earlier bravado. We were soon paying attention to every forest noise, and even though it was a bright sunny day, we were talking ourselves into a feeling of dread. After all, we were in Kakwa, world-known for its isolation and rugged solitude. Others had disappeared here.

Finally, we sat in silence until I said, "Guys, I'm going back to camp and make myself a nice hot lunch. This is total BS sitting out here getting more and more scared by the minute."

"You're scared?" Lance howled. "Are you scared, Mark?"

Mark replied, "No, but you could say I now have a heightened awareness."

Lance replied, "You guys sure make B.C. proud, eh?"

I ignored him, standing and heading back to camp. We spent the rest of the day talking to other hikers who had grand tales to tell of epic hikes and summits, and not one had seen anything even remotely scary. Not one.

Well, I lied. There was one. He as a solo hiker who came in at the end of the day. Solo hiking is not encouraged much of anywhere, and especially not in Kakwa, but we figured he was a loner type. Bears are much more likely to attack a solo hiker than a group.

But he didn't seem like such a loner when we were sitting around camp and he came over, wanting to talk to us.

"You kids be careful out there," he said, ominously. "I'm flying out tomorrow morning. Maybe you should go, too."

"Why?" I asked.

"I went a ways up Mount Sir Alexander today. I've climbed and hiked on all seven continents, and this was the first time I've seriously thought I might die."

"What happened?" asked Mark.

"Nothing happened, but when I went up, the snow was pristine. I was making first tracks. On the way back down, I saw tracks paralleling mine, going up. Something huge had climbed up behind me, and I do mean huge. It sank in three times as deep as I did in the snow, and its tracks were three times the size of mine."

"Sasquatch," Lance said knowingly.

"I didn't say that, you did," said the hiker.

"What else could it be?" Lance asked.

We discussed the missing hiker, of which the climber had been unaware. I swear I could see him turn pale even though it was nearly dark.

"You kids can come out on my charter plane. There's room."

"What about the camp hosts and everyone else in here?" I asked. "There's people in here all summer, and in the winter, too. They come in on snowmobiles from Alberta. Why is it all of a sudden so dangerous here?"

Nobody said anything for awhile, and we sat in silence. Finally, I knew Lance was thinking about flying out when he asked, "Who's your charter?"

It was the same as ours.

"I may go out tomorrow," Lance said, then added, "Why don't you guys come too? It's not much fun just wandering along the shore. I can tell already two more days of this is gonna get real boring."

"You're gonna leave us, Lance?" Mark asked.

Lance replied, "You can come too. Nobody's making you stay here, doing nothing. I'd rather be home playing baseball or just hanging around there."

I now seriously pondered whether or not to leave, and I knew Mark was, too. Finally, I said to Mark, "If you want to go, it's okay. Go ahead, but I'm staying. Even if I never leave camp, I'll be happy. This is paradise."

Lance replied, "Paradise? Yeah, Sasquatch and bear paradise. Come on, guys, let's go out. We've seen it, and we're so restricted there's nothing we can do, anyway."

We decided to sleep on it. The plane would come in at noon, so we had plenty of time to decide.

I was feeling more and more inclined to go, but then I loI was feeling more and more inclined to go, but then I looked up at the purest sweetest night sky I'd ever seen, and that's saying a lot, since I grew up in McBride, out in the middle of nowhere with no light pollution. But there was something so pure about the sky in Kakwa that I couldn't even begin to describe it, and it made me kind of wistful.

The stars were so thick it was hard to even make out the constellations as they all blended together, layer after layer of blue and white and red and yellow twinkling stars.

As I sat there in awe, it began—the aurora borealis, the northern lights, huge hanging curtains of blues and greens and golds across the sky, undulating and slowly moving.

I knew it had to be a dream. It was all too perfect. I slept like a baby that night.

Or at least I thought I did. It wasn't until the next morning and Mark asked if I'd heard the odd noise in the night that I realized something had awakened me, but I'd quickly gone back to sleep.

"What was it?" I asked.

"It sounded like a woman yelling, way off in the distance. Creepy," said Lance.

"Yeah, mountain lions do that," I said. "Sometimes porcupines will sound like that, too."

"Are there mountain lions up here?" asked Mark, then added, "Maybe it was that missing hiker."

Now, even though it was daylight, I felt a chill, but it didn't seem logical. If the hiker was in good enough shape to yell, why didn't she yell during the day until someone found her? It had to be a mountain lion.

I looked at Mark. "Lance sure changed his tune about being so brave. Are you gonna leave?"

"I think so," he replied.

"I guess I will, too," I said. "Not much fun out here alone."

What I really meant was that I wasn't brave enough to stay alone.

We broke camp and packed our gear, said our goodbyes to the camp hosts, and walked down to the beach with the climber.

Soon, we could hear the drone of the plane as it circled over, checking out the lake, then landing on the blue waters and gliding up to the shore.

The climber got into the plane, and I could tell he and the pilot were talking things over. He then yelled out, "Only room for two of you!"

So, two of us could go, but not all three. Lance was already climbing aboard, and I will say my estimation of him crashed somewhat at that moment. He was truly scared though, so I tried not to hold it against him.

Mark looked at me and shrugged, then said, "I'll stay if you want and you can go, but I think we could get our plane in to pick you up tomorrow."

At that point, I realized he had a promising future ahead as a politician or something, with his gift of double-speak. I didn't know what to say.

Mark now climbed onto the pontoon, saying, "I'll send the plane in tomorrow at noon. Watch for it. Go sleep by the cabin, or heck, go sleep *in* the cabin. The hosts are really nice, and I know they'd let you."

I stood there, disconsolate, as Mark climbed in. The plane turned, revved up the engine, and was soon cruising down the lake and into the air. I was still standing there when it became a small dot and eventually disappeared behind a tall peak.

Some friends I had. I wondered if it were a reflection on my own character to have friends who would abandon me like that. And in all honesty, I realized later, when I was off in college, where I made a few real friends, that Mark and Lance and I were friends only because we all grew up together in a small town, not because we really had that much in common.

And after this incident, I refused to have anything to do with them, but I never made an issue out of it. A month later, we were all gone from McBride anyway, off to different parts of Canada to go to school.

But as I stood there on the beach, I felt a sense of abandonment I'd never felt before or since. It was a truly profound feeling, and I've examined it many times since, but I truly felt like I was being left to die. It was an irrational feeling, I know, and there were others in the campground, so I wasn't really alone.

All I had to do was hang around camp until noon the next day, and I'd be out of there myself. The real problem was that I loved Kakwa and didn't want to leave, yet I felt afraid of the place and didn't want to stay. I guess they call this being conflicted.

I've been back to Kakwa a couple of times since, and it felt completely normal. I had no sense of fear or trepidation, even though I climbed and hiked its incredible high country for four days, though definitely not alone. I saw nor heard anything that would even vaguely begin to put me in the frame of mind I had on this first trip. Like I said before, it all felt like a dream.

I finally regained my senses and slowly walked back, lugging my gear back up to the campsite. I felt disconsolate and alone. I decided to set my tent up in the middle of the campground. If I had to be alone, I wanted people around, if that makes sense.

Once I had my camp set back up, I realized Mark had taken our pan. I had no way to cook or even make a cup of hot tea to try to drown my sorrows.

I trudged over to the hosts' cabin and explained what had happened. They were very nice and loaned me a pan, though they expressed concern about me being alone and made me promise not to hike or even go very far around the lake.

"What got into your friends that they left so early?" Jan asked.

I explained the tracks the climber had seen and the yelling during the night.

Bill looked concerned and asked, "Do you think that guy was being straightforward with you? Could he have been pulling your leg?"

"He seemed pretty serious," I answered. "He was actually quite scared."

"Well, you can sleep on our front porch," Bill said.

I was delighted by his offer and immediately took my tent back down and moved my gear to the cabin. But as soon as I laid out my sleeping bag on their porch, I felt a sense of loneliness. I suddenly wanted nothing more than to be home.

Remember, I was only 17 and hadn't been away from home much, and I knew my childhood was over and I would soon be out in the big world. All the fears at Kakwa had triggered a deep sense that maybe I wasn't ready for that world, especially if it was going to be like this.

I spent the evening fiddling with the old Pentax camera my dad had given me, trying to capture the beauty surrounding me. Believe it or not, it was a film camera and I still have the faded photos I took that day of Kakwa Lake. When I look at them now, it brings a sense of poignancy and longing for my youth.

That evening, I dreaded the darkness. Even though I was now camped on the hosts' porch, I was still outside and really had no more real security then I'd had in my tent, except that the hosts were now just on the other side of the wall.

Knowing what I know now, I personally would've invited a 17-year-old boy whose friends had abandoned him to sleep in my living room, not on my porch, but the hosts probably had no idea of the level of my anxiety, thinking that since I was from McBride, I was probably a seasoned camper.

I cooked some instant potatoes in my borrowed pan, then topped that off with some dry shredded wheat, Mark also having taken most of the food.

After eating that, I wasn't feeling so well. Mashed potatoes had, until then, been one of my favorite comfort foods, but to this day, I can't eat them, nor shredded wheat. Funny how strong some associations can be, and that night was dramatic enough that I'll never forget all the details leading up to it.

I crawled into my bag, then leaned up against the side of the cabin and immediately felt something crawling on my arm. I turned on my headlamp to see what looked like a giant spider! Of course, the shadows made it look bigger, but I came unglued, jumping out of my bag and trying to flick it off.

I'm sure it went flying into the bushes, but it now felt like everything was a spider, even the dangling strap on my headlamp. I was in a heightened state of awareness, like Mark had said he'd been the night before.

I looked for more spiders with my light, but saw nothing. But when I tried to lay back down on my pad in my bag, all I could think of was spiders.

I finally got up and sat in an old wooden chair there on the porch. You know how it is when you're tired and get something on your mind. B.C. was now the spider capitol of the world, surpassing places like the Amazon. Spiders were everywhere, just waiting for me to go to sleep so they could crawl all over me.

I sat there, then decided I would have to pitch my tent if I wanted to get any sleep at all. There would be no spiders inside my little tent, if I could just find a place in the dark to pitch it.

I suddenly felt totally defeated. How could a place of such beauty be so depressing? I just sat there in the chair, until I finally leaned my head against the side of the cabin, using my pillow to soften it, and dozed. It shows how exhausted I was that I could sleep like that.

So, there I was, sitting in the chair, wrapped in my sleeping bag, sound asleep, when I woke for no apparent reason.

My neck was stiff, but I almost went back to sleep when I heard something. It was a woman yelling. This time, unlike the previous night, I could make out what she was saying, over and over: "Help me, help me." It was clear as a bell and very unnerving.

I had no idea what I should do, so I sat there, motionless.

"Help me! Help me!"

It sounded like it was coming from out on the lake, floating across the waters, and the sound would flatten out or soften a bit, as if the breeze had turned, then come in again clearly.

"Help me! Help me!"

Could this be the missing hiker? After awhile, it finally dawned on me that it had to be some kind of trap. Something or someone seemed to be trying to lure me out there.

A chill ran down my back. I wanted to pound on the cabin door, wake up the camp hosts, but I was afraid to. I knew the noise would draw this thing to me, tell it exactly where I was.

And so, I sat there, quiet, afraid to move. The sound seemed to float from the middle of the lake, and it eventually faded away. And now I could hear a loon making its mournful sound, but I wasn't sure if it was turning into the woman's cry or was just a loon. I closed my eyes, trying to hear better.

I must've gone back to sleep, because when I opened my eyes again, dawn was breaking over the flanks of the mountains, and I could barely move, I was so stiff. My first thought was that the floatplane would soon be there, and I could leave.

I stood and stretched, stuffing my bag and pillow into the stuff sack, then started making a cup of tea. As I sat in that chair that I'd slept in all night, drinking tea, I noticed that there, not more than 30 feet away in the dim light, were two glowing eyes, eyes as red as glowing embers.

I was astonished. What animal had red eyes that glowed in the dark? I was too groggy to even be afraid. I knew bears' eyes didn't do that, so what could it be?

Then I heard the voice again. It was now very close.

"Help me. Please help me."

Was it whoever had the red eyes? They still stared at me, unblinking, and it finally dawned on me that I had to be looking at a Sasquatch, and a very large Sasquatch, judging from the height of its eyes.

Now the voice spoke yet again, and as I blinked, the eyes suddenly disappeared.

"Please, help me."

I now came to my senses and shone my headlamp where the voice was. I couldn't believe my eyes. There, slumped down against a tree, was a woman! It had to be the missing hiker!

I was still wary, and normally I would've been by her side instantly, but I needed to know where the Sasquatch was.

"Who are you?" I asked.

"I need help. I was hiking with my boyfriend. I don't know where he is. I think I have a broken arm. The pain is tremendous. Please."

Dawn was quickly pushing the shadows away, and I could see that the Sasquatch was gone.

"Stay right there," I said in my best rocket-scientist fashion, as I knew she wasn't going anywhere. I began banging on the cabin door, and in a moment a light came on.

"It's me, Al," I yelled. "We need help—the missing hiker is here!"

The door quickly opened, and Bill came out. He quickly assessed the situation and carefully helped the woman inside. She was gaunt and looked like she was in shock. Jan was soon on the satellite phone, calling for help, and before I knew it, a helicopter was there, picking up the hiker. It all happened so fast, and she was gone before I could even really register everything that had happened, but I knew she was in good hands.

Later that same day, at noon, I stood on the beach, waiting for the bush plane, too exhausted to even appreciate the shimmering glacial blue of Lake Kakwa. I sat down on a rock and waited—and I waited and waited and finally lay down in the warm sand and slept. The events of the previous night had taken their toll.

It was late afternoon when I awoke, refreshed. I knew that just because Mark had said he'd send a plane didn't mean he could actually schedule it. I would have to wait for tomorrow and our regularly scheduled plane before I could leave. One more night at Lake Kakwa. I felt dispirited.

I lugged my gear back up to camp yet again and asked a large group of mountain bikers that had just come in if I could camp with them, telling them I was scared and didn't want to camp alone. At that point, I didn't care if everyone thought I was a coward.

They were from Edmonton, and not only did they let me set up my tent in the middle of their camp, they insisted I have some of their big spaghetti dinner, complete with salad and homemade rolls. After dinner, they built a fire and we all sat around and talked.

They seemed happy to learn I was from McBride, and asked me all kinds of questions about mountain biking around the area. We talked late into the night, when I finally gave up and crawled into my tent. I felt very secure there surrounded by my new friends and was soon fast asleep. I dreamed I was home, in my own bed, dreaming that I was in Kakwa.

The next day, as I waited again on the beach for my plane, I was joined by two hikers who asked if there would be room for them to fly out. I said I thought there was, but why were they leaving before their own scheduled charter would arrive?

They looked grim and were tight-lipped, saying only that they needed to go home due to some unplanned event there. It was all rather vague, and I wondered how they'd gotten word of this event in the backcountry of Kakwa, but I didn't ask.

The plane was on time, and as it took to the sky above the beach, I looked down and said, "Sasquatch tracks!"

Of course, I really didn't see any from that height, but the looks on my fellow travelers' faces told me all I needed to know about the real reason for their early exit.

I read in the news later that the missing woman hiker had somehow managed to make her way six miles down the mountain with a broken arm, but was rapidly recovering. She'd managed to hike across a ridge and down a different drainage than where everyone had been looking. Everyone said it was a miracle she had survived, as she'd somehow managed to make it across the lake.

As unbelievable as it seemed, I suspected she'd had help.

2. The Sasquatch Paleontologist

This story came from a fellow who Sarah and I met at the head-quarters of Yoho National Park, which is adjacent to the more famous Banff National Park. Yoho is famous for being the loca-tion of the Burgess Shale, one of the world's most important fossil finds.

This fellow was studying the fossil exhibit there in the head-quarters, and when he saw we were likewise interested (Sarah's a geologist), we all began talking. We really hit it off, and over lunch, he told the following story.

—Rusty

I don't know if you've ever heard of the Royal Tyrrell Mu-seum in Drumheller, Alberta, but it's one of Canada's finest museums and a big tourist attraction. Lots of families make it a destination for their vacation. Kids love the place, as do most adults.

It's basically a dinosaur museum, although that's a little misleading, as it also has invertebrate fossils from the fa-mous Burgess Shale in Yoho National Park, as well as fossils from the Pleistocene. So, its exhibits span a long time, most of the Earth's prehistory.

But even though this museum has world-class fossils such as the coal black bones of the T-Rex called "Black Beauty," it's also world-class in the way the fossils are displayed. At times it's almost like being in an art museum, the way everything's perfectly lit and arranged.

Anyway, not to get too sidetracked on the museum, as you can find out more about it on the internet, but just to mention it as being the backdrop to my family's annual vacations. Lots of Canadians visit the Rockies or go to Vancouver for vacations, but my family always went to Drumheller and the museum. And it's also home to some of the worst hordes of mosquitoes I've ever seen, but that's another story.

We always spent two weeks each summer there helping as volunteers. My dad was a banker, and this is how he wanted to spend his vacation, plus he thought it would be good for us three kids. My mom enjoyed it too, plus she knew my dad had wanted to be a paleontologist, so she did it for him.

It was the happiest times of our family life, and I'll always treasure the memories—except one, and I don't think "treasure" is the right word—"try to forget" is more like it.

We usually did stuff at the museum, primarily in the bone lab. We'd been trained in removing fossils from their rock matrices, and it was painstaking and slow work, so the museum was always happy to have trained volunteers. Of course, this could get monotonous, so we would break it up with helping set up displays and things like that. We all learned so much, and it was fascinating. We had a small camp trailer and would stay at a nearby RV park.

I especially liked the Burgess Shale exhibit, as it was like walking through the ocean when the strangest creatures lived, like Hallucigenia and Pikaia. I always gravitated to that exhibit, weird as it was.

Well, one year, my dad decided we needed to try something different, something outdoors and more physical, so he arranged for us to park our trailer at a site the museum was excavating out in the badlands near Drumheller in Horseshoe Canyon.

We were very excited at the opportunity to actually help dig up bones like the ones we'd been working on at the museum. We felt like little Indiana Joneses. Yes, my parents were happily raising three little nerds, even though none of us became paleontologists. My brother's an insurance adjuster and my sister's a nurse, and I'm in administration for Canadian Provincial Parks.

So, that summer we hauled our trailer out to the dig site and set up camp. There were several paleontologists there—a couple from various universities and one from the museum—plus a dozen or so students who were getting college credit for digging.

This was going to be a special vacation, I could just feel it in my bones. Another thing that made it special was that we were able to bring our dog, Dippy, when usually we had to leave him with a dogsitter.

Dippy was an unusual dog. Nobody could figure out what breed he was, and I think it's because he was a bunch of breeds mixed together—a mutt.

Dippy was short for Diplodocus, a big dinosaur with a long neck and long tale that fed on tree leaves. Dippy had a long neck and tail, and thus his name, though he didn't eat leaves.

Being on a bone dig is actually mostly a lot of hard work and isn't a bit glamorous, so we found out. But the thought of maybe discovering a new species or something significant made it exciting in its own way, in spite of mostly just digging in the ground, then extracting whatever you found and wrapping it for transportation to the museum.

And the mosquitoes kept us from slowing down too much. If you stopped, they would eat you alive, even though we all wore mosquito nets and long-sleeved shirts and pants. They didn't bother Dippy, fortunately, probably because of his long hair.

We were working in the colorful badlands eroded out by the Red Deer River, different layers of pinks and whites and tans, very pretty, down in a small valley.

We'd been there about a week and a half when everyone left to go into town for some kind of visiting display. It was a two-day grand opening for some new dinosaur from China, and the people who had found it would be there to talk about it.

We kids were given the choice of going or staying, and partly because of Dippy and not being sure what to do with him while in a motel, we decided to stay. Besides, having a dino dig all to ourselves was a big deal to us. We would be in charge for once, though in charge of what, I don't know—each other, maybe, though none of us were very good at following orders, unless it was from our parents. And we had strict orders to stay at camp, though I have no idea where our parents thought we might go with no transportation.

So, everyone left and there we were, at our dino bone camp, just the three of us and Dippy. It felt very cool, and we pretended we were famous paleontologists out on a dig in the wilds of Argentina, home to many major fossil finds.

This was fun for awhile, then we got bored with it and went back to work. We did take more breaks than usual, but we generally didn't have much to do except dig, so we dug.

Everyone else had left early that morning, and by mid-afternoon, the novelty had worn off. Connie, my sister, was kind of over on one side of the dig by herself, and Joey and I were both digging on a nearby slope.

I was engrossed in trying to chip a small bone out of a rock when I saw a shadow above me. Looking up, I could see Connie standing on the slope above me. She looked at me, then sat down by me and whispered, "Tommy, some-body's watching us."

"How can you tell?" I casually looked around but saw nothing.

"Can't you feel it?" she asked.

I sat there for a while, silent, but felt nothing.

"Where are they?" I asked.

"I don't know."

Now Joey had joined us.

"Something feels creepy all of a sudden," he said.

"That's just because Connie's making you feel that way," I replied.

"No, I felt it before she came over. It's like something's watching us. It made the hair on the back of my neck stand up."

"Dippy isn't worried, and he's a good guard dog," I said, pointing to where he was curled up in the dirt, sleeping.

"I'm going to work over here by you guys," Connie said.

We all got back to work, when suddenly I felt it. We were definitely being watched. How could I tell? I can't explain it, it was just a feeling, some kind of intuition. Maybe a sixth sense left over from when we humans were more wild and had to watch out for predators.

OK, we were pretty scared, but being budding scientists, we wanted some kind of evidence it wasn't just in our heads.

We all three stood there in silence, casually looking around, but trying not to be real obvious about it. If there were someone spying on us, we wanted to be cool and not let them know, as we figured this would somehow give us an advantage.

Finally, when we saw nothing and yet still felt weird, like we were still being watched, I whispered, "Get to the trailer, but don't run or act scared."

As the oldest, I was in charge any time our parents left us, and my brother and sister were used to listening to me. They knew mom and dad would always stand behind me if there were any questions about our behavior, as I had a good credibility rating.

So, off we shuffled to the trailer, afraid to look behind us, but also wanting to look and see if we were being followed. My brother was last inside, behind Dippy, and he almost slammed the door, he was so nervous. I reached over and locked it behind him.

Keep in mind that this was just a small travel trailer, the kind you see parked behind people's garages with weeds growing all around the wheels, nothing special or expensive, kind of just a tin can. It certainly wouldn't have provided us much safety, as it would've been pretty easy to break into.

We pulled the curtains closed and sat there around the little dinette, saying nothing. It was only mid-afternoon, and our parents and the dig crew wouldn't be back until sometime the next day. We had a long time to ponder life on our own in the backcountry of Horseshoe Canyon.

Finally, Connie whispered, "I know there's something malevolent out there. You don't have the hair on your neck stand up for no reason."

"Yeah," Joey chimed in, "And we all three felt it."

"Look," I said, "It seems to me that about the only dangerous thing out here, other than the gigantic mosquitoes, would be bone thieves. You suppose someone knew everyone was leaving and is now planning on stealing the bones we've been working on?"

"How they would do that is beyond me," Connie said, "Since they're still in the rock. It would take a gorilla to carry off even the little bit of stuff we've loosened up."

"Maybe the bone thieves aren't aware of that and are coming in to see what they can steal. Maybe they weren't planning on us staying behind," Joey said.

"We could be in a very dangerous situation," I said, sounding all authoritative when I was really feeling like a chicken. "I think we should just stay inside until everyone comes back."

"That's not going to work," Connie said. "First of all, what if we need to use the bathroom? The Port-a-Potty is clear on the other side of the dig. And we're going to sit in here all night scared to death in the dark, wondering what's out there? I vote we go right back out and let whoever it is know there's nothing here for them."

"How would you do that?" asked Joey.

"We could just yell at them, 'Hey, there's nothing here. No bones worth taking,' then get back to work."

"You're always the pragmatic one," I replied wryly.

Well, this went on for awhile, the three of us arguing, like we always did, until Connie finally made us feel like cowards, and we decided to take action.

We would climb a small hill back behind the trailer where we could see out. If there were someone parked down the road trying to hide, we could see them, as well as all around the dig site.

Where we'd been digging was kind of in a bowl, and climbing up out of it would either reveal who was out there or reassure us that our imaginations were indeed getting the best of us.

This was great, except the execution was kind of hard, as we were all still scared stiff, but we finally opened the door and took off up the hill. We basically ran up it and were winded by the time we got to the top, where we got down on our stomachs behind some bushes and peered down at the dig site below. I still laugh when I think of that—anyone watching us could easily see us run up there and hide.

We crouched down there for some time and saw nothing. I was about ready to write it all off to our overactive imaginations when I thought I saw something move back behind a big rock near the dig. And now Dippy, who had been crouched down with us, as well as a dog can crouch, began growling.

"Someone's hiding over there," I said quietly, pointing to the rock. We crouched down even lower and watched. Before long, a head poked out from above the rock. It took a minute for me to register what I was seeing. Whoever it was, they were very tall to be able to look out over that rock.

Joey said what I was thinking, "They must be really tall to see over the rock. It's big."

We watched in silence as whoever it was now stepped out from behind the rock. They either hadn't seen us run up the hill or didn't care if we saw them. I put my hand around Dippy's muzzle to keep him quiet.

And as they now became totally visible to us, no one said a word. We all lay there in shock at what we were seeing.

Finally, Connie said, "Wow, that's a good costume."

Joey replied, "A good way to not be recognized when out thieving."

I said, "I don't think it's a costume, guys. If you watch its legs, you can see the muscles rippling."

"I was worried about that," Joey said nervously.

"What is it?" Connie asked, and I could tell she was trying not to cry.

"It looks to be a Sasquatch," I answered, now actually shaking but trying to hide it.

"It's someone playing a joke on us," Joey said. "Someone in a gorilla costume."

We lapsed back into silence. The creature now walked over to where we'd been digging and started looking around. It was so large and so strong-looking I knew it had to be real. A costume could never look so genuine. And it looked almost regal, the way it carried itself.

"It acts like it's interested in what we're doing," Joey whispered.

"Maybe it's mad because we're out here in its territory," Connie said.

We watched in silence, as it was close enough we worried it might hear us, even though we were whispering. It now got down on its knees and examined the rocks where we'd been digging and removing the bones, running its hands all around the indentations and then picking up some of our tools and examining them.

Finally, it stood and looked directly up the hill to where we hid. I knew it could see us. It was a terrifying thing, knowing this huge creature could see us huddling down on the ground, trying to hide from it like a bunch of cowards.

I hoped it would see we were young and leave us alone. I figured if it were mad at humans for disturbing its territory it might cut us some slack, kind of like you would a puppy that has an accident inside the house.

I whispered, "You can't hold youth to much."

"What?" Connie asked.

"We're just kids," I replied.

"You're not making any sense," Joey said.

I looked at my brother and sister, and I wanted to cry. They were young, and being so brave, and maybe this thing would come right up here and kill us all. I wondered what everyone would think had happened, especially my parents, when they found our bodies. I did my best not to cry, trying to set a good example for the others.

Now the Sasquatch turned and started back towards the big rock it had been hiding behind. I sighed, hoping it was leaving and would let us be. In retrospect, kids are much more accepting of things. If I were to see something like that now, I would probably get PTSD and have to visit a shrink twice a day. But we just kind of accepted its existence, although this doesn't mean we weren't scared to death.

As the creature went back behind the rock, we all breathed a sigh of relief. Hopefully it would go away and leave us alone. But I knew we'd be spending a sleepless night in the little trailer, regardless. I still held Dippy's muzzle as he watched the creature, his hackles up.

But now I could hear something that sounded a little like groaning, and soon the big rock began to move. We watched as the big beast pushed that huge rock until it took on its own momentum and rolled right smack onto the place where our dig was, smashing our tools and stopping with a sickening crunching sound.

I wanted to yell out, "Hey, why'd you do that?" but I kept still. I was amazed at the strength the creature had, and I didn't want to draw its attention to us.

"Why'd it go and ruin our dig?" Joey muttered under his breath.

Now the Sasquatch turned and walked away with huge strides, soon disappearing down the canyon into the shrubs and trees. I knew it had made some kind of statement, and I wasn't about to ask it for an interpretation. Its meaning seemed pretty clear—it wasn't too happy about us being there.

We stayed crouched on the hill for some time, until my legs got sore and I needed to stand up, which I did. I looked as far as I could see, but saw nothing.

"It's gone," I said. "Let's go back down."

We ran for the trailer, Dippy at our heels, where we jumped inside and locked the door. I knew it would be a long night, wondering if the Sasquatch would come back, though all was quiet and the creature didn't return. Apparently it was happy with the message it had left in the form of the big rock.

We felt better the next day, even though we were all sleep-deprived, and we even managed to get up the courage to go examine the dig site and see how much damage had been done.

It was pretty major, for the rock had rolled right smack on top of the major portion of the dig. I could see no way anyone could remove it without a backhoe.

In the meantime, I wandered over to where the rock had been. It was kind of strange, but it looked like maybe it had been covering up some sort of odd-looking fossil, something stained with iron oxide. I traced around it with my fingers, and it looked to be some sort of intact skeleton.

I called the others over, and we all stood there dumb-founded. It was about then that our parents showed up, Dippy running out to meet their truck.

My mom and dad got out and walked over to the big rock, scratching their heads.

"You kids better have a good explanation for this one," my dad said.

"There must've been an earthquake," my mom replied. "That rock's too big for those kids to move."

We called my parents over to look at the fossil embedded in the matrix where the big rock had sat. Soon, the rest of the dig crew had arrived, and everyone was standing around looking at either the big rock or the fossil.

One of the paleontologists got down on his knees and closely examined the bones.

"This looks to be a Therizinosaurus," he said reverently. "We've found Therizinosaur relatives here in Alberta, but never one of the feathered guys. If that's what it really is, it will be quite a find."

Now my dad took me aside and asked, "What happened here, Tommy? Surely you kids have some insight into all this."

I didn't think he would believe me if I told the truth, so I just shrugged my shoulders. But just then, Joey and Connie came over and motioned for me and my dad to follow them.

They led us down the valley a ways, then stopped and pointed at the soft ground. There, in perfect form, was a Sasquatch track.

Dad turned white. Now he got the picture.

We talked about what had happened that night in the trailer over dinner, and the next day, my parents hitched up the trailer, and we left. I don't know if they told the others about the Sasquatch or not, but it was our last outing with the museum. After that, we started visiting the national parks on our vacations.

It turned out that the fossil was indeed a Therizinosaurus, the first ever found there, and the museum eventually put it on display.

And that poor Sasquatch never did get credit for the find.

3. The Water's Deep

Sarah and I met this gal, who asked not to be named, at a wine tasting near the town of Kelowna, in British Columbia's famous Okanagan Valley (of which you'll soon hear more). She lived a little bit south, in the town of Osoyoos, and when she learned of our interest in Sasquatch, she invited us to visit, saying she had a story for us. We stopped at her place on our way home, and as we sipped her wonderful home-brewed peach ale, she regaled us with the following story.

—Rusty

I've been an avid reader of mysteries since I was a kid and first discovered Agatha Christie, but sometimes real-life mysteries I'm not so fond of. They seem to leave me feeling like something's off and things are out of order.

The world is full of such mysteries, and I know some people love trying to solve them, but I prefer the kind where I know the answer will be had by the end of the book.

And so, it would be just my luck to get involved in a real-life mystery, much to my chagrin. And I would give just about anything to know what happened in this particular case, though I know I never will—I'll just never know the answer.

Like all good mysteries, one has to start at the beginning. This one didn't really start with my retirement and purchase of a little travel trailer, but without those events, I wouldn't have been in the place I was to know about this mysterious event. I'll explain.

I'd been looking forward to my retirement for a couple of years, planning things out, and my main theme was to travel a lot. With that in mind, I spent many of my weekends looking at small travel trailers, ones I could pull with my little Toyota Tacoma pickup. In retrospect, I think I enjoyed the looking and planning almost as much as the actual retirement.

I finally settled on a trailer made in British Columbia, in a town not too far from where I live here in Osoyoos. I travelled to the factory and took a tour and was immediately sold on the quality and feel.

I bought a model they had on the lot, a two-year old trailer that someone had traded in for a new one. I felt very lucky, as these trailers were hard to come by, and getting one custom built took a year or more. I would prefer not to name the brand, as it would be a huge clue as to the person this story is about, and I think his family might object.

I retired six months after buying the trailer and was all set to go. As I said, I mention the trailer because that's what got me involved in this mystery.

Because the factory was a small, family-run business, there weren't a lot of these trailers produced, and therefore one always took notice when seeing another on the road.

There was a sort of camaraderie among fellow owners and even an online forum where one could post recent sightings. A lot of people had the names of their trailers in lettering on the back, names like "Bluebird" and "Freedom."

So, I was bound to notice these trailers once I was retired and on the road, and I even made friends with a few other owners. We felt like we were kind of an exclusive bunch, but in a good way, not in a snobbish way.

Well, after I retired, I ended up spending a lot of time touring British Columbia and Alberta. I had always had a goal of camping in each of the provincial parks in these two provinces, and since I lived in B.C., it seemed like a reasonable goal. So, I made a list and an itinerary of all the parks and had at it.

I would go out for a month or two at a time, then go home and regroup and download all my photos, that kind of thing, then start on the next leg of the journey. Through it all, I met a number of other owners of this type of trailer, always super nice folks. I got to where I would look for such trailers in each campground.

So, this is how I got involved in the mystery, because if I hadn't bought this trailer, I wouldn't have noticed the fellow who owned one in the park I was in, and I wouldn't have stopped to talk to him.

Honestly, I really wish at this point in time, as much as I love my trailer, I hadn't bought it and could still be ignorant of it all. I'm ready to sell it and not travel any more.

Well, now that you have a bit of perspective, here's what happened.

I was on my way home to Osoyoos, and I wanted to stay at a particular park on the way back. I'd rather not say which park to help protect the guy's identity, and you'll soon see why, but it was in central B.C., in the Okanagan Valley, a place known for its produce, including fruits.

This particular provincial park was on a large lake and very beautiful, or so I'd been told by others who had stayed there, and I'd saved it for the trip home, as it was about a half day's drive from my house.

So, once I got there, I pulled in after dark and was real worried I wouldn't be able to find a place, but I happened to find a spot on the far side of the campground, away from the lake. This was fine by me, as that way I'd be farther from the mosquitoes, though they really weren't a problem this late in the year (September).

As I was entering the campground, I noticed a trailer just like mine in one of the camp spots. I figured I would get a good night's sleep and then go introduce myself to the trailer's owner the next day, assuming he or she hadn't left.

I slept well, though I was awakened once during the night by what sounded a little like a foghorn. Being on a large lake, I thought maybe someone was out in the dark in a boat or something.

I'm not much of a water person (Osoyoos is in one of Canada's rare deserts), and I don't know anything about boats, so I didn't think much about it at the time. The noise had a deep resonant sound to it. I only heard it that one time, but I think it was a portent of things to come.

The next day, I wandered over to the trailer and introduced myself to a nice-looking older man with red hair. He had just retired, like me, and we both had a great time talking about our trailers and the life of retirement.

I visited with him for some time, drinking tea and eating some scones he'd bought in some little gourmet shop in the town of Salmon Arm. We really hit it off, and I promised I'd come back in the evening, and we'd build a fire and talk some more. The nice thing about Canadian provincial parks is most of them provide free wood. I'd bring some nice wine I'd bought in Kelowna, which is also in the Okanagan Valley.

I spent the rest of the day cleaning my trailer, reading a book (a mystery, of course), and generally just being lazy. As the day wore on, I put together a small basket of some cheeses, a baguette, and that nice bottle of red wine. It was nearly dark when I grabbed a jacket and flashlight and headed for Jim's trailer (not his real name, of course).

The park was heavily wooded and had only a few people camped there, as it was the end of the tourist season. This particular trip would be my last one for the year, and apparently the majority of people had gone home, judging by how empty the park was.

A lot of my friends are snowbirds and winter over in Arizona, but I always just stay home, as Osoyoos has a really moderate climate, especially for Canada, and doesn't get much snow.

Anyway, that evening, I walked down the gravel road and was soon at Jim's trailer. He sat outside in his anti-gravity chair (portable recliner), pushed back, watching the last rays of sun lighting the clouds high above.

He apparently didn't see me, because when I said hello, he nearly jumped out of his skin and almost tipped over.

There was still enough light that I could see his face was white as a sheet, and it seemed odd to me that I would scare him like that, especially since he was expecting me.

"You OK?" I asked.

He said he was fine, but had heard someone in the trees over by the lakeshore talking and had thought they'd walked over to his camp without him knowing. He had a camp site only about 50 feet from the water's edge.

I was kind of puzzled that someone entering his camp would scare him so badly, but I said nothing.

We had another pleasant talk, and the cheese and wine really hit the spot. I asked him about the canoe leaning against his picnic table, and he said he'd been a lifelong waterdog and loved being on the water.

"I love to canoe—it's how I escape reality," Jim added. "I was a horticulturalist in my former life, specializing in turf grasses. You know, the sods they use for golf courses and such. It's kind of funny, but I know more about grass than most people know about their own kids, I would guess. I've spent a lot of time researching natural grasses, too, to see if we could grow a more hardy strain than the standard bluegrasses."

We talked more about grasses, then Jim asked about my previous profession. I was an antique dealer, and we talked about that for awhile, then got back onto the subject of grasses.

Jim said, "You know, this place is really strange. I canoed around the lake a couple of days ago and found a big meadow. It was a different green from the rest of the grasses around the lake, so I had to investigate. I'll be darned if it wasn't a square type of grass. Never seen anything like it, and it looked like someone was tending it. There wasn't one weed in it, and it was as lush as could be. But there wasn't a road into it or anything, so I don't know how anyone could be getting back in there, unless they canoed in. But it had a fenced perimeter, though it was really rough, made of dead trees and branches."

Jim shook his head, then added, "I'm going to canoe back in there and get a sample of it to take back to the university and see if anyone knows what it is. It looks like a new species to me."

We talked on and on about different things, and the evening soon turned into pitch darkness, the kind you get in deep arboreal forests where the sky is blocked by tall trees.

I was really enjoying our visit and kept sipping wine, and, in fact, I had a little too much. I'm not a heavy drinker, and when it was time to go, I wasn't sure I could find my way back.

Jim was sober, and he took one look at me and insisted he drive me to my trailer, even though it wasn't all that far away.

I assured him I'd be fine, but he looked concerned and basically refused to let me walk back. I finally accepted his ride, even though it took only a couple of minutes to get me back to my trailer. I think, after all I now know, that he was afraid for my sake because of something else he knew about and I didn't.

"I'm really not that tipsy," I said as I got out of his pickup. "But thanks anyway."

What Jim said next really struck me later, when I realized it was a piece of the puzzle, a clue to the mystery. At the time he said it, there was no mystery yet, so I didn't ask him to elaborate. It just seemed kind of an odd thing to say.

"The water's deep," he said, then added, "I think it comes up under that meadow and irrigates it somehow. Thanks for a nice evening. See you tomorrow, I hope."

He then drove away, and I went inside and was soon fast asleep.

That night, I woke, as someone was outside my trailer talking. I lay there and listened for awhile, wondering why they were out there in the middle of the night, but the voices quickly died out, and I figured it was someone on their way to the restroom who had stopped by my trailer to talk for a minute.

The next morning, I had a bit of a headache, so I lazed around and drank a lot of coffee until it finally went away. I vowed to not drink so much wine again.

Around noon, I wandered over to see if Jim were around, but his trailer was empty and his pickup was gone, the canoe still leaning against the picnic table. I figured he'd gone sightseeing or into the nearby town or something, and I proceeded to start walking around the lake.

It was a huge lake and very overgrown with shrubs and big trees in places, so after awhile, I had to turn back, as the little trail I'd been following petered out.

I started back, then decided to take a photo and turned around for the shot. To my shock, I caught a glimpse of something brown quickly stepping into the bushes, as if it were following me and didn't expect me to suddenly turn around.

This gave me pause. Most of B.C. is bear country, and this thick forest was perfect bear habitat, including grizzlies, the last thing I wanted to run into, especially out here all alone. What had I been thinking, walking out here like this without even carrying bear spray?

I turned and walked back at a brisk pace, though I actually wanted to run. Every so often, I would turn again to see if I were being followed, but I didn't see anything and was soon at the campground, though it felt like it took forever.

Now, I would normally feel very safe in a campground, even without it being full of people. Most bears avoid humans, especially in the daylight. But I was still weirded out that one would follow me like that, and I no longer felt safe, even there.

I made a cup of hot tea and tried to kick back and read the book I'd been enjoying, but every few minutes I'd feel a sense of anxiety. I knew I was being silly, but somehow I couldn't make the feeling go away.

I went inside my trailer and continued to try to read, but the feeling felt even stronger, as I could no longer see around me, being indoors. Something could be right outside, and even though I was probably safe, I wouldn't even know it was there.

Let me add that by this time, I had camped in quite a few provincial parks, some fairly remote and empty, and I'd never felt any sense of fear whatsoever, especially in broad daylight. This particular park wasn't that far from town, and there were other people around, and yet I was beginning to feel true anxiety, and what was worse, it wouldn't go away.

It was getting along towards mid-afternoon when Jim drove up. I was half afraid to go outside, so I invited him to come in.

He sat down at my little dinette and began talking up a storm, telling me about a little road he'd just driven that went around the other side of the lake, though one had to drive clear back into town to get onto it. I gathered by this that he liked to get out and explore.

"What was interesting," he said, "Was that I could see someone walking along the opposite shore from where I was, and there was something big and brown following them. I got out my binoculars, and it sure didn't look like a bear, as it was walking upright."

I was shocked, knowing he'd seen me—it had to be. What on Earth could've been following me?

What Jim said next was another piece of the mystery, I'm sure, though I had no way at the time to know what he meant.

"I'm from Vancouver, and I've read about these things. I'm not so sure I want to camp any more, which is a shame, considering I spent half my life waiting to retire so I could get out and camp and explore. I had no idea they really existed, but what's even more unsettling is I had no idea they could mess with your mind like they do."

"What in hellsbells are you talking about?" I asked, not really wanting to know. I was beginning to question his sanity, as well as mine. And I had also made an important decision, one based on a hunch, but not really on any facts.

Jim sat quietly, as if he didn't want to answer my question. Finally, I said, "I'm feeling pretty unsettled here. I'm going to take off."

"Right now?"

"Right now," I answered, standing and beginning to put things away. "It's been nice meeting you, but this place is starting to feel very strange to me. Maybe you might want to head out yourself."

"They won't hurt you, you know," Jim said.

"You just said you're considering not camping any more," I reminded him.

"I'm going to stay one more night, then leave. They tried to lure me out of my trailer last night, but I'm on to them."

"Why would they do that if they're harmless?" I asked, shivering. I wasn't sure if he was nuts or not, but my own feelings and what I thought I'd seen out on the trail made me think he was sane and being honest, and there really was something strange out there.

"I don't know," was all he said.

I now tried to talk him into leaving. I was getting a worse and worse feeling from all this, but he was not to be persuaded and soon went back to his trailer. By the time I'd put all my outdoor stuff away and hitched up, it was nearly dark, but I knew I would rather drive in the dark than stay.

I was now beginning to feel like I was being watched, and I felt a huge sense of relief when I drove out of the park, not even stopping to say goodbye to Jim.

The further I got away from the place, the better I felt. I finally reached the nearest large town and pulled over in the parking lot of a big-box store and spent the night, along with a few other campers in RVs. I felt very safe there and slept well, feeling a huge sense of relief to be away from the park.

I was home by noon the next day, but the feeling that something was off stuck with me for a few days. I knew I would never return to that particular park.

A week later, I read something that confirmed my suspicions about the place. The headline was: "Vancouver Man Goes Missing in Provincial Park," and beneath it was a photo of a trailer just like mine.

The article described my friend Jim and how he'd just mysteriously disappeared. The RCMP (Royal Canadian Mounted Police) had activated search and rescue, but no trace could be found, and nothing in his trailer looked touched.

It was a mystery. The lake was thoroughly searched in case he'd drowned, but nothing was found. He had just disappeared into thin air, and even search dogs could find no trace. One of the park managers said in the article that bears had been particularly active in the park that fall.

I kept my eye on the news, and sure enough, a week later, his body was found by a canoeist, floating in the lake. Jim's canoe was still in his camp. No one was sure why someone that was a good swimmer would just fall into the lake and drown like that. It was a mystery, though I personally didn't think he fell in.

The paper said that his trailer would be taken back to the factory by the people that manufactured it, as Jim's family, who all lived in Ontario, had sold it back to them.

Not long after that, a friend of mine from the U.S. drove up to B.C. and bought it. He lived in Portland, Oregon and had heard me talk about how much I liked these trailers, plus the company would help him export it into the United States, which would make the purchase much easier. Sometimes exporting something into the U.S. can be a real pain, as the paperwork is really tricky, since Canada doesn't have actual titles like the U.S. does.

But I'm getting sidetracked. Of course I hadn't told my friend anything about how I'd met the previous owner of the trailer, as it was all something I just wanted to forget. I still had occasional feelings of panic when I even thought about being there in that same park where he'd disappeared, not to mention the odd things he'd said.

My friend stopped by Osoyoos with the trailer on his way back to Oregon. He wanted to catch up since I hadn't seen him for awhile, plus have me show him everything about the trailer and how to use its water and electrical systems.

We had gone through everything, and I was now showing him how to put out the awning, when something fell off the top as I unrolled it.

"What the heck?" I said, picking up a small bundle of half-dried grass tied with a piece of string. It was a sort of square grass, like nothing I'd ever seen.

My friend asked about it, and I told him it must've been unknowingly on top of the awning when it was rolled up. I somehow knew Jim had put it there, hiding it from someone or something. It was the sample he'd said he was going to get. Whoever had moved the trailer hadn't known it was there when they rolled up the awning.

I shivered. Had Jim angered what I now suspected were Sasquatches when he'd entered what was maybe part of their carefully tended food supply? Had they somehow suspected his intentions and known it would mean nothing but further intrusion by humans? Had they then drowned him in the lake?

I didn't know.

Like I said, it's a mystery, one I'll never be able to solve, even though I still have the grass bundle, carefully wrapped in wax paper in the back of my refrigerator. I keep thinking I should take it in for analysis by some horticulturalist, but I know I probably won't.

Just as some mysteries will never be solved, some things are better left alone.

4. The Sasquatch Catskinner

Oh boy, what a story this is! Its teller, William, joined one of my guided fly-fishing trips when I was just starting out as a guide. I think we were on the Madison River in Montana.

I've kept this story in my archives for a number of years, not quite sure I believed it. But I've decided to go ahead and include it here, for if nothing else, it shows the fine tradition loggers have for storytelling. And who knows, just maybe it's true. Stranger things have happened in the world of Bigfoot.

—Rusty

I'm William, and I was born and raised in Quesnel, B.C. It's pronounced "kwe-nell" and is named after a French explorer. It was the center of the Cariboo Gold Rush, but it's also a big logging area, with pulp mills and a plywood plant. It's been called the most concentrated wood-products manu-facturing area in North America.

I'm not a logger, but my dad and granddad both were, so I grew up in that culture, so to speak. The culture of logging—well, I guess you could call it a culture, of sorts, or maybe a lifestyle. There's a logger stereotype, and a lot of it is based on facts. These guys work hard and they're not rich, but they would do anything to help someone in need. Most of them are a bit rough around the edges but have hearts of gold.

But logging has really hit B.C. hard. People drive through the province and see mile after mile of thick arboreal forests and think it's a pristine place. Much of it is, but there are also lots of places where the entire forest has been removed, clearcut into oblivion.

This changes the whole ecosystem, but it also alters the way runoff flows. I don't know if they still log the way they did when my granddad and dad worked in the industry, but I hope they're more responsible now. Clearcutting can result in mudflows, as we'll see in this story.

Anyway, I grew up with loggers, and I sometimes think I had a perfect childhood. I'll never forget when my dad would take me to the logging camps when he was running supplies, and how great everyone was.

Sometimes, if the camp was a long ways out, I would get to spend the night in my dad's big army surplus canvas tent. We slept on cots, and I remember many a time I worried that a bear would come in and drag me away.

I think this had actually happened to someone, or at least the guys told the story around the campfire. Just like your campfire stories, Rusty—they would build big fires (they had lots of wood of available) and get to drinking on special occasions when they couldn't go home, like Thanksgiving.

I heard a number of bear stories around these fires as a kid, but what really bothered me were the Sasquatch tales. Most of them were of the varieties of a Sasquatch rolling fuel barrels down the hill or vandalizing camp while everyone was out working. A few of the guys had actually seen them, but I don't think all of them believed in them, as I recall one of the guys getting ridiculed when he told about an encounter.

It was probably in their best interest to not believe, given they were out there in the woods all day. Fear of Sasquatch wasn't a good thing when you needed to concentrate on the task at hand with such a dangerous job.

And so, hearing the stories, I grew up believing in Sasquatch. I recall asking my dad if he'd ever seen one, and he said no, but he knew they existed.

When I was a teen, I developed other interests and quit going to the camps with my dad, which I think made him feel bad, yet he'd always told me he didn't want me to be a logger because it was too dangerous.

But I do remember our last trip out together, though neither of us realized it would be the last. We bounced around in his old truck on our way out—the logging roads could be pretty rough. And at one point we stopped because he thought he had a flat tire. As he was checking it out, I thought I saw something brown move in the trees, and when I told him he jumped right back into the truck.

The tire wasn't flat, just low, and we got the heck out of there. That's when he told me he knew Sasquatch was real, because his dad, my grandpa, had seen one.

Now, you have to know my grandpa to really understand. Unlike a lot of the loggers, he never drank or cussed, and he was a religious man, very devout and as honest and straightforward as they come. Like those loggers' hearts, his word was as good as gold. So if he said he'd seen a Sasquatch, you can be guaranteed he had, or at least something he thought was one.

My dad said that he'd been about my age at the time, and he'll never forget the day my gramps came home from the logging camp early. He had quit his job and said he had no intention of ever going back out.

Of course, after a few weeks of looking around and finding nothing else, he went back to logging, but only because he had a family to feed and no choice. He always hated it after that.

So, here's the story my dad told me that day, the same story my gramps told both him and my grandma that day he quit his logging job and came home early.

My gramps was a catskinner, a bulldozer operator. He would push logs around and clean up dead scrub and build roads, whatever needed doing. He was good at it and could make that cat do whatever he wanted, whether moving something big or something little. He was a crackerjack catskinner.

It was a skilled job, though after this incident, I once heard him laughingly tell my mom that it didn't take much to run a cat because he'd seen a Sasquatch do it.

Anyway, this was somewhere in the hills around Quesnel. The terrain was hilly to mountainous, with big stands of fir, balsam and spruce. It had been raining for a few days and the whole logging camp was shut down because of this, and everyone was anxious to get back to work, as they didn't get paid if they weren't working.

The rain finally stopped, and Gramps got out on his bulldozer, his D9 Caterpillar. He was cutting a new road out into the timber, and the rest of the camp was depending on him so they could get out there and start cutting a new section of forest. There was some pressure on him, but my grandpa was a go-getter anyway and usually the first on the job.

So, even though it was a bit wet and soggy, Gramps got out on that cat and got to work. He said it was muddy, but only about the top two feet or so, and when he got down lower with his blade he was able to push the mud and dirt out of the way and build road.

He was making pretty good time when he came to a slope. He stopped, wondering if it was too muddy to cut across it and keep going. It was the top of a steep little draw, a somewhat gentle slope but steep enough that he was a bit worried.

As he sat there, studying things, he saw movement in the trees below him. He thought it was a deer and didn't pay it much mind, but then he heard something whacking, wood on wood, "thump thump." Now he was paying attention.

Maybe it was a big old grizzly breaking logs to get to the termites or whatever they eat, grubs, I guess. It was now about lunchtime, so Gramps pulled out his sack lunch and sat there on that old D9, munching away on a ham sandwich, thinking about the recent rains and that slope he needed to cut across.

He heard the thumping noise again, but this time it was rhythmic. "Thump-thump, thump-thump." That struck him as kind of weird. He finished up his lunch and pulled out a cigar when he heard another "thump thump" in the distance. Now, the closer one seemed to answer, "thump thump."

His first thought was that some of the guys were pulling a prank on him. Logging camps did get pretty boring, and the guys made up their own entertainment, and pranking was an accepted form of such, as long as you didn't cross the line.

So, he figured the guys were bored, waiting for him to finish the road so they could get back in there and get to work. He yelled out, "I'm real scared, guys. Must be some Sassys out here." He always called Sasquatch, "Sassy."

The whacking stopped, so he figured he'd been right, they were pulling a prank. He got down off the cat and pulled off his shovel, walked a ways out on the slope, and dug a hole.

Yup, about a foot of wet soil, then it was dry under that. This seemed safe enough to him, so he fired 'er up and got to work building that road.

As he was working, he thought he saw something big and brown again, down below him. Gramps was moving real slow, being extremely careful, as he knew there was a chance the cat could start sliding down that muddy slope. But he figured as long as he was blading out the mud ahead of him and staying on dry ground, he'd be okay.

Well, he figured wrong. He said he suddenly had a sinking feeling as he felt the cat began to slide sideways down the slope, just a few feet and very slowly. He gunned it in reverse, trying to get back onto firm ground, but it was too late, it had started really sliding, and he was rapidly losing control. He said it was like trying to drive a toboggan.

As he looked up, he saw the entire slope starting to go! He had triggered a mudslide, and the weight of that big cat was enough to get things going. It wasn't a huge slide yet, just the top couple of feet moving down the hill, but Gramps knew that it would be fairly deep by the time it got to the bottom of the draw.

It was at that point that Gramps bailed. He jumped off the cat and managed to get to the side of the slide and into the trees before it really got going.

That whole slope was now coming down, rumbling and trees breaking, and Gramps stood there in shock as he watched it go, taking rocks and shrubs and trees in slow motion right down that draw, the Caterpillar riding on it like a surfer, slowly turning. He expected it to sink, but it didn't, it just slid down with the rest of the debris.

Now Gramps watched in even greater shock as he saw the big brown thing. He could see it down the slope trying to outrun the slide, and even though the slide was going in slow motion, the thing couldn't outrun it. Gramps didn't understand why it didn't head for the edge, like he had.

The cat was in the front of the slide, still moving down and slowly turning around, when the brown thing jumped onto it. That was when Gramps figured out what it was because he could gauge its size relative to the Caterpillar, and it was big.

It wasn't a bear, but a Sassy! Last thing Gramps saw was the Sassy riding the cat as it slowly turned, following the draw, on down out of sight.

Gramps said he ran all the way back to camp, scared to death. He never mentioned the Sassy to anyone, but told them about the slide.

They went out to see where the cat had ended up and after they all scrambled down the edge of the draw, they found it at the bottom, unscathed, sitting there, half buried in mud and debris.

A few days later, after things had dried up and they decided it was safe enough, they brought in another cat, cutting a path through the trees, then digging and pulling the half-buried cat out. It had suffered very little damage and they were able to salvage it, clean it up, and continue using it.

Gramps never said a word to anyone about the Sasquatch, but a couple of the other guys noticed its muddy footprints and gave Gramps a strange look, but he never said a word.

Gramps said he probably would've been fired if he hadn't quit, as the boss said he'd been negligent in cutting the road through unsafe conditions, but heck, that's how they always worked back then. You just got the job done, regardless. And that particular guy had wanted to give Gramps' job to some relative anyway, so Gramps said to have at it.

When he went back to logging, he went to work for another company, and he refused to work alone after that, so he started felling trees, hand logging, a job that usually required several guys. He finally retired, but he always told my dad to never work alone.

So that's the story of the Sasquatch catskinner, just how my gramps told it.

5. The Sasquatch Matchmaker

This is a sad story, in spite of the somewhat flippant title I gave it, but it also has a happy ending (for all but the Sasquatch, that is).

Tim and I met on a fly-fishing trip on the banks of the Green River, which drains much of Wyoming's northern Rockies and becomes one of Utah's big desert rivers. It wasn't so mighty where we fished, though, along its shore near Pinedale, Wyoming, where it's still more of a stream.

I really enjoyed fishing with Tim, and I must say he had one of the more unique stories of how he and his wife met.

—Rusty

I think this is may be one of the more unusual ways to meet a future spouse. Meeting someone in a tourist parking lot isn't that unusual in itself, but the event that triggered us talking to one another was quite unusual—so much so that when people ask how Joni and I met, we just say in a parking lot and let it go at that.

I'm Tim, and when this all happened, I was in my early thirties and still not married, as I put my career as an ER doc on the front burner and never had time for a relationship. I did have a few short-term affairs, but women quickly got tired of my lifestyle and called me a workaholic, saying I was married to my job.

In a way, it was true, as I always wanted to be a doctor, but coming from a humble background, I had to earn every minute of it.

I'd finally achieved my goal at a fairly young age, and I could actually say I loved my job, though it could be stressful. I would decompress by reading travel blogs and by looking at maps and planning my own dream trip of a lifetime, to drive the Alcan highway, now called the Alaska Highway.

The highway itself technically starts at Dawson Creek, B.C., but for me, the trip really began when I crossed the Canadian border. That was all new territory for me, as I'd never been through there before.

I was such a greenhorn traveler that I was nervous crossing the border station in Washington, and I recall wishing I had a cigarette. I had smoked for about two weeks as a college freshman and quickly realized how self-destructive it was and quit. Can you imagine an ER doc wanting a cigarette? After all the smoking-induced trauma and disease we deal with?

Okay, I'm getting totally off track here, which I have a tendency to do. Sometimes I'll start trying to educate the patient on their problem and will end up having a nice conversation on just about anything else. My patients say I have a nice bedside manner, but I'm really just interested in people and their lives. And I'm still off track, so back to Joni, love of my life.

I had bought a nice Ford pickup and put a used camper on it, as everyone said that was the best way to travel to Alaska. You had your bed with you so you could stop anywhere you wanted, which was good, as a lot of the long road up there is fairly remote and lacking in amenities, and I didn't like motels, anyway.

I crossed the border at Creston and headed on over to Invermere, as I wanted to see the famous Canadian Rockies on my trip up. I would go to Radium Hot Springs and camp in Kootenay National Park, then go see Lake Louise and all the famous places near Banff, then head up the famous Icefields Parkway to Jasper.

I knew this portion of the trip would be very crowded with tourists, but I was willing to deal with this to be able to see some of the most stunning mountains in the world. Living in Seattle at the time, I'd spent plenty of time in the Cascades in Washington, and they're truly unique and beautiful, but there's something about the size of the Canadian Rockies that takes your breath away.

They're not that tall in comparison to other mountains, like the Colorado Rockies, but they start lower in elevation so you get more sheer height. And their sedimentary layers make for some really interesting topography.

I camped at Invermere, a nice town by a big lake, then drove on to Radium Hot Springs and turned east. Wow, was I in heaven the minute I entered Kootenay National Park with its glacial blue and green rivers! I then travelled on to the sites around Banff. I could go on and on here, but you just need to go see it to understand.

So, on with the story. I'd spent several days in that area and had finally started up the Icefields Parkway, which goes through both Banff and Jasper national parks.

Now, Canada has national parks just like the U.S., but it also has tons of provincial parks. I'm not really sure what the difference is, as some provincial parks are as epic as the national parks, and you can usually camp in both. Maybe it's the way they're managed and used. But I'm getting sidetracked again.

The Icefields Parkway is a smooth four-lane highway that cuts right through the Rockies from Lake Louise to Jasper, a distance of about 140 miles. It goes through a long valley for miles, following a beautiful wide but shallow glacial river that's a pale milky blue, then eventually climbs to the Columbia Glacial Field, and thus its name, the Icefields Parkway.

At one place, you're just across the road from the Athabascan Glacier, which appears to be hundreds of feet thick. There's a big tourist center there where you can buy tickets to go out on the glacier in these giant snowcats. The glacier is quite a sight, and you can also hike out on it, though there are signs everywhere saying how dangerous it is.

On down the road just a ways from the big glacier center is a pull off, and I stopped there to get some photos. This lookout is right across from some huge cliffs coming off the mountain where the edge of the glacier hangs and huge waterfalls drop down from the glacial melt. By huge, I mean the size of the ones you see in Yosemite, and there are about a half dozen coming off the cliffs, some on a second band of rocks beneath the first.

The falls are far enough away that you need binoculars to really see them well, so I got out my high-powered glasses and leaned against the front of my truck and started scanning the cliff bands. My gosh, that glacier is thick. It looks to be at least 100 feet, and you could see far above its terminal edge, where it hung down the mountain.

That in itself was pretty dramatic, but the falls were beyond spectacular. I could imagine the roar they must have made if one were closer. It was a very dramatic scene.

I love stuff like this, the forces and power of nature, and I was so enthralled that I didn't even notice when a small car pulled up next to me. I did notice a very pretty woman getting out of the car, but I was soon back to my binoculars.

Finally, she asked me what I was looking at. You could see these distant falls only if someone pointed them out to you, as they blended into the snowy cliffs from a distance. I handed her my binoculars, and she was just as spellbound as I had been.

While she was viewing the scene, I noticed a black spot moving on the glacier above the falls. I told her to check it out. It had to be a rock slowly slipping down the glacier, but it was hard to figure out the mechanics of this, as a rock would be stuck in the snow and ice, not moving, plus I then realized it was going more sideways.

"It looks like a big grizzly bear," she replied, handing back the binoculars.

I took a look and was amazed. It was indeed some kind of large bear, and it appeared to be trying to cross the glacier. It looked like it was far enough from the lip of the glacier that it was in no danger. What a day, to see a grizzly on a glacier in Canada! Not something you see every day back in Seattle, for sure.

I handed the glasses back to this very pretty woman, and as she watched the bear, I began to watch her. She seemed very intelligent, though how I could tell is beyond me, and that, to me, was more important than looks in a partner, because they were going to be the one helping you get through life.

But I swear I wasn't consciously thinking about this, it was just on a subconscious level, but I knew I wanted her to stick around long enough to get to know her better.

I noticed her plates were from B.C., so I asked what part of the province she was from. She was from Victoria and was on vacation. I didn't want to pry, so I didn't ask any more questions, but I remember being happy that she lived fairly close to Seattle.

I took the binoculars back, watching this bear, and it stood on its hind legs. I could now feel the hair on my arms stand straight up and a chill go down my back. The thing no longer looked like a bear. I handed her the glasses, wanting to see her reaction.

"My God," she said. "What is that thing?"

The few people I've told this story to all ask how we could see this thing from that distance, but let me tell you these were very powerful Nikon binoculars with excellent resolution.

I looked again, and I could see it had very long arms and was built like a linebacker. It now proceeded to walk upright across the glacier, and I held my breath, for it was getting closer to the lip.

"It's too close to the edge, whatever it is," I said.

"It's a Sasquatch," she replied matter-of-factly.

I ignored what she'd just said. To me, Bigfoot was a total myth, one I'd heard plenty about, living in Washington. I thought the whole concept was silly. But what I was seeing really didn't look like a bear.

"What's it trying to do, anyway?" I asked.

"Probably just get across the glacier, but it acts like it's not really aware of how close it is to the edge," Joni replied.

"That glacier's so thick it could probably walk right on the edge and be okay," I surmised.

"The Sasquatch looks really heavy," Joni noted.

"What would you guess?" I asked.

"Maybe 600 or 800 pounds. It's huge."

We talked like this, all the while holding our breath while taking turns with the binoculars. Finally, I said, "I'm Tim."

"I'm Joni," she replied. "Nice to meet you."

We watched some more, spellbound. Joni had the glasses and was watching when it happened. In retrospect, I'm glad I didn't see it, but I also wish she hadn't, as it really messed with her mind. In fact, it still does somewhat after 10 years.

Joni gasped, and I could barely see what looked like a huge chunk of ice break from the glacier's lip, and, as if in slow motion, come tumbling down that sheer cliff, huge chunks of ice breaking off and flying through the air alongside the huge waterfalls.

Now she started saying, "Oh no! Oh no!" Her hands clutched onto those binoculars like a lifeline, and she kept saying "Oh no!" over and over.

She stood watching for the longest time, and when she finally handed the binoculars to me, I could see tears. I didn't have to ask, I knew the avalanche had taken the Sasquatch with it.

I scanned the base of the cliffs where the chunks of ice had landed, but saw nothing but a rubble field of snow, with the waterfalls coming down onto it. I knew there was virtually no chance anything could have lived through such chaos.

We both stood in silence. Had we really seen a Sasquatch, and not only that, but one fall to its death? What were the odds of that? I couldn't even imagine.

I put my binoculars into their case and quietly asked Joni if she would mind sticking around long enough to describe to me in detail what she'd seen. I offered to make her a cup of tea, so we climbed into the back of my camper and set at my little dinette, drinking tea and talking, looking out the window at the distant waterfalls.

I never mentioned to Joni that I was a doctor, as it's been my experience that women who might not be at all interested in me suddenly are, as they imagine a wealthy lifestyle. I'm far from wealthy, but I get by OK.

Funny thing is, I never asked her about what she did either. I didn't even asked if she were married.

After a couple of hours of talk, we headed our separate ways on down the road, even though we were both headed to Jasper. We did exchange cell numbers.

I got to Jasper a few hours later when my phone rang. I didn't recognize the number, and cell phone service in Canada is a couple of dollars a minute if you're on a U.S. plan, which I was, so I didn't answer.

Whoever it was had left a message, so I finally got curious enough to listen to it. It was Joni. Would I like to meet her for dinner in Jasper at the Raven Bistro? She was staying at a friend's, and I could park my camper there for the night if I wanted.

Jasper's a busy tourist town, and as beautiful as it is, it's just not my cup of tea. I had planned on keeping on going, but something said to have dinner. I needed to eat anyway, right? I was tired of soup and PBJ sandwiches.

I called her back and met her at the restaurant, and all I can say was it was all downhill from there. What I mean is, I never made it to Alaska, but I did come to explore the city of Victoria and its surroundings quite well, staying at Joni's house after we left Jasper. We did finally travel to Alaska, but years later.

We were married a year later, and come to find out, Joni is also a doctor, a pediatrician. I moved to Victoria for a few years, then missed the U.S., so we both got jobs in Kalispell, Montana in a hospital there.

We're close enough to her family in Victoria that we can visit when we want, and since most of my family lives in New Mexico, that's not terribly far either.

And what about the Sasquatch? Well, we beat that subject to death talking about it, and we both read everything we could about them. Nothing can convince us that what we saw that day up on the glacier was anything else.

But what a unique way to meet your spouse, eh?

6. The Loon of Lac La Hache

I've heard lots of stories about how Bigfoot or Sasquatch imitates bird and animal calls, but this is one of the better ones, in my opinion. Of course, there's also the story later in this book about a Sasquatch imitating people ("The Mount Robson Whisperer"), an act that probably takes a little more linguistic finesse.

In any case, this story came from a super nice couple, Buddy and Jenny, who are both avid fly-fishers. They came on one of my wilder fishing trips—wild not only because of this story, but also because we got caught in one of the more dramatic lightning storms I've ever seen and were happy to survive.

—Rusty

This is a crazy story, but I swear it's true, and my wife Jenny will vouch for me, as she was there. I feel like a fool telling it, but Rusty, you're one of the few people I think might get it. So onward I go.

Jenny and I were doing a weekend at a nearby provincial Park, Lac La Hache. That means hatchet lake, but I'm not sure where that name came from, although someone told me it was named that when a long-ago trapper lost his only hatchet when chopping a hole in the frozen lake to ice fish.

It's a fairly large lake just a bit north of the town of Lac La Hache, going towards the much bigger town of Williams Lake on Highway 97.

We didn't much care for the back side of the park, as it was dark and in the tall timber, big Douglas firs. In fact, most of the park was like that. It's a very nice park, don't get me wrong, but we were tent camping and preferred to be where we could see out more.

Does that make any sense at all? You're in a tent but you want to be able to see out. Go figure. Anyway, I think being in the tent made us not want to be in thick dark timber, as B.C. has lots of bears.

So, we opted to stay on the side of the campground that fronts out onto the highway, plus you can see the lake from there, as it sets down the hill on the other side of the highway and the park is higher than the road. Being above the lake may have played a part in how easily we could hear things down there.

Anyway, we set up camp and made dinner, then sat in our chairs and watched twilight fall. A few boats were coming in late, and it was cool to see their lights floating across the lake as it reflected the deep blue of the sky and the reds of the sunset. It was a perfectly tranquil evening and we were really enjoying it.

Well, you know how it is when you get to talking. You bundle up and are nice and cozy and the stars come out and you just don't want to go to bed. I don't remember what we talked about, probably a bit of everything, knowing us, and it was getting late.

It had to be midnight when we heard a loon cry coming from far across the lake. There's no sound on earth that can make you feel as lonesome, like you're the last human alive in the deep wilderness. It's a beautiful hauntingly eerie sound.

We had heard loons before and sat there, lost in our own thoughts, listening. Now, coming more from this end of the lake sounded another loon, closer and clearer. There's something quintessentially northern about the cry of the loon, and it has an effect that's hard to describe. It's very cool, at least until the loon then starts to sound like maybe it's dying, which this particular loon started to do.

Jenny and I looked at each other in the dark. What had started out as a perfectly good loon cry turned into a sort of gurgling noise.

"You think something's wrong with it?" I asked.

"I've heard them make some pretty weird sounds," Jenny answered, "But nothing like that."

We sat, silent, listening, as the faraway loon cried out, its sound carrying across the lake. Now the nearby loon tried again, started out just fine, then deteriorating into a coughing noise.

"Can loons cough?" Jenny asked.

"I've never heard any kind of bird cough," I replied.

We sat a bit longer, then the chill came in so we climbed into our tent and warm sleeping bags. We could hear the loon on the lake below make one last attempt, which was almost perfect, then we both dozed off.

The next morning, we were up early and had breakfast, our camp chores done before the sun was up. We wanted to go boating or whatever people do at Lac La Hache.

It was a beautiful day, and we ended up just sitting on the boat dock, watching boats come and go, people fishing and waterskiing. We then had a nice dinner back at our camp. After that, we decided to take an evening walk down on the nearby lakeshore, where we'd heard the confused loon the night before. Jenny was worried we would find its poor little bedraggled body, as it sounded like it was near death.

We walked along, finding loon tracks everywhere, but fortunately no injured or dead one. But as we rounded the shore directly under our camp across the highway, we found something that was truly odd.

There was a deep pit dug into the sand, maybe four feet deep and eight feet long, and whatever had dug it had apparently climbed in and out of it, filling it with leaves and ferns.

The sand all around the pit was so trampled I couldn't make out any real tracks, but Jen pointed to something that vaguely looked like a toe track. It was big, and I decided it had to be the impression of part of a stick, but she swore it was a toe.

"This looks like a giant bed," Jenny remarked.

"And it has sort of an odd smell to it, Jen," I replied. "I don't like the looks of this. It could be a bear's bed or worse yet, from the smell, maybe where a bear decided to cache a deer or something."

"There's nothing here, though," Jenny replied.

"Well, maybe it dragged it away, but I think we should turn back."

I stood and looked towards our camp and could barely make out the top of our orange tent. We were camped directly above the hole, and all that separated us from it was the highway and a broad slope going down to the lake.

We walked back, our paces not as leisurely as going out, and I kept looking back nervously.

"That kind of creeped you out, eh, Buddy?" Jenny asked.

"Yes, and one of the most dangerous things in the world is walking up on a bear's cache. Remember that young guy killed not too long ago down at Towgatee Pass in Wyoming? He was doing forest research and walked onto a cache. He was killed."

"Yeah, that was sad. But what we saw looks more like a big bed to me," Jen replied. "Maybe that sickly loon fell into it in the dark, though I would think they could see better than that."

We were soon back in camp, once again sitting in our camp chairs and enjoying the evening. We were tired and went to bed early, dropping into sleep immediately.

It must've been around 2 a.m. when something woke me. I was very still, but heard nothing. Finally, Jen whispered, "Did you hear that, Buddy?"

"Something woke me, but I'm not sure what," I replied.

Just then, I could hear a loon crying in the distance. From just below our camp came a reply. This time, The call was perfect, but something was off.

"That's too loud to be a bird," Jen said.

"I'm feeling kind of freaked out," I said. "In a manly way, of course," I added, trying to make light of my fears.

Now the distant loon sounded out and it was much closer.

"The loon's coming in, and it's in danger," Jen said.

"How do you know?"

The loon below our camp cried out.

I answered my own question. "You're right, Jen, it's too loud to be a bird. This is creepy."

Jen replied with concern, "It's calling in the other loon, maybe to kill it. We have to do something."

"Jenny, it's 2 a.m., and besides, what could we do?"

But I was too late. Jenny had unzipped the tent fly and was heading for the car.

"Hurry up, Buddy," she said.

I knew she had a plan, but I had no idea what it was. But I was all for getting into the safety of the car at that point, so I followed her.

She started up the car and drove out the park gate and onto the highway. When she was directly below our camp, she pulled onto the edge of the road.

"This isn't really where I'd like to stop," I told her.

"Quiet," she commanded, cutting the engine.

We were now parked above the slope going down to the lake, directly above the pit we'd found. Jen rolled down her window, and we sat for a while, listening.

No loons, just silence.

"Well, I guess the sound of the car put an end to whatever was calling in the loon," I said. "Let's go back to camp."

"No, let's wait awhile," she replied.

We sat there so long I started dozing off. Suddenly, Jen poked me.

"The loon's not that far away. It just called out. It's looking for its mate."

As she said it, directly below us came the sound we'd heard earlier. It was now obviously no loon, for it bellowed out the loon sound like a bull elephant imitating a loon.

"I think it's whatever dug that pit, Jen," I said nervously. "And if that's the case, it's much bigger than us. What if it decides to come up the bank?"

"Maybe it digs pits, then sits in them and calls loons in, catching them in its mouth when they fall in," I added.

"That seems rather far-fetched," Jen said.

Now the far loon was crying out, much closer.

Just then, Jen sat on the horn. It was so loud and so sudden it almost scared me right out of my pants. She honked and honked, and I was afraid she would have everyone in the park awake and coming to see what was wrong, then she finally stopped.

The silence seemed deafening after all the noise. But we didn't sit there long when we heard a new noise.

Something was crashing through the brush between us and the highway, coming directly our way.

"Jen, start the car. Let's get out of here! You've made someone really big really mad."

Jenny quickly started the car and swung around across the highway just in time to see a large form come running through the edge of the brush, across the highway, and straight up the slope into Lac La Hache Provincial Park.

The campground was busy with talk the next morning of the previous night's events—someone honking and honking down by the highway, which woke a number of people, then something huge crashing through the park.

A few campers said they'd seen it, and it was a Sasquatch. Jen and I had sat in the car the rest of the night, too scared to even crawl into our tent. When dawn came, we made ourselves some breakfast, took down our camp, and were soon gone, but not until talking to a few other campers, who were also heading out.

So, that's the last time we camped there, pretty as it is. Jen always says she saved the life of a loon that night, and to this day, when I hear the call of the loon, I wonder what it really is.

7. The Plein-Air Bigfoot

My wife, Sarah, loves art and was really intrigued by this story when we first heard it. We met its teller in an art gallery in the town of Golden, British Columbia, where Sarah was admiring the woman's very talented landscape paintings.

We actually ended up buying one of her paintings of the Bugaboos, which are near Golden, and after we all talked for some time, she told us the following story. She asked that her name not be used and that we change the places so she wouldn't be recognized, as she's a pretty well-known artist.

—Rusty

I used to be a heli-guide in the Bugaboos in British Columbia. I have since done well enough with my art that I could retire from that and focus entirely on my gallery in Golden.

What do helicopter guiding and art have in common? Well, maybe more than one might think.

When people hear the term heli-guide, they automatically think heli-skiing, where you get lifted into pristine wilderness to ski out. Yes, there is heli-skiing in the Bugaboos, but that's not at all what I guided. My deal was a bit different.

I was a struggling artist, so I came up with this idea to make money, which I desperately needed. It was either figure out some kind of art-related income or get a real job.

There were plenty of jobs where I lived near Banff, but they were all tourist related and pretty low paying, things like working at the counter restaurant in Lake Louise. I wasn't all that young anymore, and jobs like that take it out of you, both physically and mentally. I wanted to do something different.

I had a couple of friends who are heli-ski guides, and they helped spur my new career. I would be a heli-guide, but my helicopter tours would be in the summer, not the winter. I figured there were lots of people who would prefer to see the Canadian Rockies in their summer beauty, and my helicopter trips would cater to those who wanted to get into the Canadian high country without all the planning and effort that backpacking would take, plus you wouldn't need to be in that kind of shape on my tours.

Since I was an artist, I wagered there were enough kindred souls who would pay to be flown into some remote spot to do a day's worth of plein-air painting. I would also provide instruction as part of the deal.

I felt it was an idea of pure genius, one that could make me a good solid summer income, and I could then spend the winters doing what I loved—painting. In addition, I would get to meet other artists and also maybe even get to do some plein-air painting myself. I knew nice landscape paintings of such awesome country would sell well to tourists back in the numerous galleries in Banff, the ultimate crazy Canadian tourist town.

I knew the logistics would be killer, and getting permits would be tough. I had no money, but lots of time and my friends to help me. They knew the helicopter pilots and maybe could talk one into working when I had clients, getting paid by the trip.

To make a long story short, I pulled it off. I had a lot of help, but I had to do my own website and advertising, and getting a permit from the Canadian government wasn't easy. But since there were already people heli-skiing in the Bugaboos, I decided my chances of getting a permit there would be easier.

It wasn't easy work, making all the arrangements, and my first summer as a heli-guide was a near disaster, as it seemed that if something could go wrong, it would. It's a miracle I pulled it off, and after running the business for five years, I sold it and made enough to basically retire, though I live very frugally and also make decent money from my landscape paintings.

Anyway, with that background, fast forward to my last summer with the business. Things were going very smoothly, and I'd managed to attract enough artists that I was able to offer a special tour with a well-known landscape painter.

I don't want to name this particular artist, so let me just say that if you're at all into landscapes, you would probably recognize her name. She played a part in the story.

I thought the price I was asking for this special trip was exorbitant, and I couldn't believe it filled up in the first few days.

Once everyone gets up in the high mountains, they set up their easels wherever they want to paint, some facing the mountains, others the little lake, etc. We always would paint in this little bowl where the view of the Bugaboo Spire was just tremendous, and it was always fun to see the expression on people's faces when they saw where we were landing.

I hope I didn't get too long-winded with all that, but I wanted you to know how this was all set up. So, here we were, myself, a well-known artist (I'll call her "Sue"), and my generally well-heeled clients who were paying a fortune for all this, most of who were women. I'm not sure why, but lots of women are into plein air, maybe because they're nature lovers.

There were several men, and one guy in particular named Jeremy ended up playing the center role in the event, though I'm sure he would've preferred otherwise, but it was all luck, based entirely on the fact that he decided to place his easel facing a stand of trees.

I think he regretted that decision, but maybe not. I didn't get to talk to him very long afterwards, but he did send me an email later saying he'd really enjoyed his once-in-a-lifetime adventure, but that maybe next time I should forewarn people about what could happen.

I got a kick out of that one, like I'd had any inkling of what could happen myself. I was just happy he didn't ask for his money back.

So anyway, everyone had set up their easels and were enjoying being in the Canadian high country. Sue and I were walking around talking to each person, giving them tips about how to paint what they were seeing.

I can't begin to describe what it's like to be up in the Bugaboos, some of the most spectacular scenery on Earth.

If you get a chance, take a look at some photos on the internet. They're these huge granite spires in the Purcell Mountains surrounded by immense snowfields and glaciers. Of course, we didn't fly up into the actual spires, but instead set down by a small glacial lake with the spires in the background. Even in summer, it was cold up there, so everyone wore jackets.

It was late morning, and I'd been walking around checking out everyone's paintings, giving them tips, in general somewhat amazed at how talented this particular group was. The fellow I mentioned earlier, Jeremy, had set up on a small rise looking down into the thick forest.

His painting was progressing nicely—it was of the forest with huge spires in the distance (I'm not sure, but if I recall correctly, it was maybe Snowflake Spire). As I was studying his painting, I noticed something odd in the center, in the trees a bit. It looked like a face.

"That's really nice work, Jeremy," I said, then pointed out some techniques for him to try out. I looked again at the dark face in his painting, back in the trees. It was odd. I looked toward where he was painting, but there was no face.

Maybe he likes to add stuff in, I thought, maybe he was into adding a bit of the psychological or something like that. I said nothing and continued on to the next client.

Typically, most of my clients are intermediate painters, though I did get some beginners and occasionally experts who just wanted to get into the Canadian high country and paint. I would normally end up learning more from them than they did from me. Jeremy seem to be one of the latter, an accomplished painter.

I wandered back to him, intrigued by the face he'd added into what was an otherwise glorious painting. He was obviously a professional.

Now Sue was also standing by Jeremy, eyeing his painting. She said, "Jeremy, what is this face in your painting? Does it have some special meaning?"

Jeremy replied, "I don't know. I'm just painting what I see."

We both squinted, looking into the thick trees, then looking at each other questioningly. Jeremy was now back at work, intent on his painting, and Sue begin offering him tips, so I moved on, perplexed.

I walked around, making sure everyone was happy, offering tips, then gradually making my way back to Jeremy.

The face in the painting now had details. It was strange, resembling a cross between a human and an ape.

"Very interesting," I said, hoping Jeremy would offer up some meaning.

"It is weird, isn't it?" he responded, then kept painting, working on the colors in a rock in the foreground.

I finally decided he had to be joking around, though he seemed very serious. I climbed up higher on the edge of the bowl and stood on a rock where I could see down into the trees and watched for some time, but saw nothing. I finally went back down to where Jeremy was.

I was totally intrigued by his painting, but also puzzled. I'd never had anyone couple a plein-air painting with fantasy.

Jeremy looked up and said, "I know you're wondering about my painting, but I really do just paint what I see. He's not there now. He takes a break, then comes back."

The face in Jeremy's painting now had the beginnings of a body. I wasn't sure what to say, so I kind of lamely asked, "What are your goals for this painting?"

Jeremy replied, "I'm a portrait painter by trade, and I want to branch out, get away from people. I'd like to move exclusively to landscapes."

I knew he was from Los Angeles, so I asked, "You're going to do landscapes in L.A.?"

Jeremy replied, "Oh, I'm planning on moving to San Diego. I think I can do ocean paintings and sell them to tourists."

"Kind of what I do, except mine are Canadian," I replied. "But will your paintings have elements of fantasy like this one? It's a very unusual combination."

Jeremy looked at me, puzzled, then responded, "Once again, I'm just painting what I see."

"Oh," I said lamely. "You certainly have a much better imagination than I do."

I looked again into the trees, but saw no dark figure.

Because Jeremy had set up at the upper edge of the small bowl we were in, I couldn't see into the trees without standing where he did or climbing up higher.

I realized I was ignoring the other clients, so I walked around some more. By the time I was ready to go back to Jeremy, Sue had just returned from him. She pulled me aside.

"That guy, Jeremy, he sure has an eclectic approach to landscape painting. I swear he's painted a Sasquatch into a very nice painting. He's very talented, but he's pretty much ruined a beautiful painting with his weird imagination."

"Agreed," I replied. "But he's paying good money to have us critique it, so I'm wondering if saying so might be in his best interest. But I don't feel qualified to do so. He's a much better painter than I am. Maybe you would be the one, since you have a lot more experience and expertise."

"Yeah, maybe I should say something. But who knows, maybe some Sasquatch fan would buy it. Sure limits his audience, though."

"Agreed," I replied.

It was time for lunch, and I was putting out a gourmet spread on a big portable picnic table surrounded with camp chairs. The joys of having a helicopter bring you in— you could haul around stuff like that.

Sue walked over and said, "You know, this is a lot of fun. Being instantly transported into a place like this, having a gourmet lunch set up for you, meeting great people— what's not to like?"

"And getting paid to do it," I replied, smiling.

"It's unbelievable," she said. "I'd be open to more of this, if you want."

"I'm sure we can work something out," I replied. "We sure had an awesome turnout for this."

I then walked around and told everyone lunch was served. Jeremy seemed reluctant to leave his easel.

"Can you save me some?" he asked. "I want to finish this before your friend leaves."

"What friend?" I asked.

"The guy back in the trees in the suit."

"Guy in the trees?" I was shocked.

"Yes, the one I've been painting, your friend."

"My friend?" I didn't know what to say. Maybe it wasn't all his imagination after all.

"Isn't he part of the class?" Jeremy asked. "I think it's a great idea introducing an unexpected (though ugly, if I might say so) element into such a beautiful scene. Of course, I know it's a suit, but it sure seems real."

I looked at his painting—he'd completed all but the feet.

"I'll save you lunch, but don't be long, please."

I walked away, still in shock. Was he indeed painting exactly what he saw? I went to Sue and told her what Jeremy had said.

She replied, "He's joking around. He has to be."

"I thought so initially, but he seems so serious about it," I answered, not sure what to think.

We ate lunch, everyone laughing and talking about their work and how great this all was, and I kind of forgot about Jeremy for awhile. When I remembered and went to where he'd been painting, I could see his easel was still there, but he was gone.

I figured he'd probably stepped into the trees to pee or something, and I went back to the lunch group. But after a few more minutes, I decided to go check on him again.

There was no sign of him anywhere, just his easel with the painting on it. I noticed the feet were now complete. It was a perfect rendition of how I imagined a Sasquatch would look.

I yelled for him, but got no reply. Now I was seriously worried. I motioned for Sue to come over. When I told her what was going on, she looked scared.

"Not a word to the others," I said. "He's probably got himself lost while taking a break."

"What should we do?" Sue asked.

"I'm going to radio the helicopter to come up early. We're supposed to leave in a couple of hours anyway. We can't go anywhere without Jeremy. Eric will fly over and look for him."

Now Sue started fussing and worrying, pacing around.

"Look," I said. "Go on over and finish lunch. Not a word to anyone. We'll find him. It's hard to hide from a helicopter. But we don't want to upset our clients."

Sue went back over to the others while I climbed a small rise, scanning the countryside around me. No sign of Jeremy. I pulled out my satellite phone and called the helicopter pilot, explaining we had a lost client.

This was a first for me and something I hadn't prepared for. Who would expect someone to get lost when all they were supposed to do was stand around and paint? I had visions of search and rescue taking out a body. I've always been good at imagining the worst, but this had never even seemed like a remote possibility before this.

Eric was in the air above us in about 30 minutes, flying out of Invermere, and he was soon flying low, scanning, looking for Jeremy.

He finally returned and landed, and I ran over to the helicopter.

"I can't find any sign of him," Eric said. "You'd think someone up here could navigate their way back using the peaks as landmarks."

I was now really concerned. "What should we do?"

"Maybe it's time to call out search and rescue," Eric said, reading my mind. "We want to get them up here before it gets dark. It gets pretty cold up here at night, and this is wild country. We need to find him before he gets himself really lost."

I walked over to where Sue and the others were. She had everyone over at the picnic table and was giving a mini lecture on some landscape painting techniques. No one noticed that Jeremy was missing, and she'd explained the helicopter by telling them it had come up early and was doing a reconnaissance (which was true, in a way).

Just then, I heard a howl coming from the forest. At first, I thought it had to be Jeremy, but then it dawned on me that it could possibly be a Sasquatch.

My blood ran cold, and I wondered if the Sasquatch hadn't been real and somehow had something to do with Jeremy's disappearance.

But just then, Jeremy stumbled from the trees, yelling with excitement. I ran down to where he was, and he was so happy to have found us that he was whooping and hollering.

I was beside myself with relief, and I could tell Eric was, too. Sue waved from over by the picnic table.

Since the others had no idea Jeremy had disappeared in the first place, they kept on talking and laughing. I didn't say much at the time, but later, after we all got back to the airport, I took Jeremy aside and asked him what had happened.

He said, "I was almost finished with the painting. All I had left was the feet, and the guy was standing kind of back in the trees, his feet hidden in the grass. So I motioned for him to come out, which he did, standing at the edge of the forest watching me. I then painted his feet, amazed at how big they were, and now that I could see him better, I was really amazed at how realistic his costume was."

He paused, thinking, then added, "I really thought that this was one of your staff, adding a wildlife element to things to spice them up. I thought it was pure genius, getting us to think outside the box. Well, this fellow started motioning like I had, to come over, so I left my easel. I thought he had something he wanted to show me. As I walked towards him, he turned and disappeared into the trees, so I followed him.

Once I got in there, I got kind of scared. I thought about how you instructors seemed perplexed by my painting, then I recalled hearing about this thing when I was a kid— this thing called Bigfoot, though you Canadians call him Sasquatch. It hadn't even dawned on me until then that this might be exactly that, a Bigfoot, and it had watched me from the trees all morning while I painted. I think it was just curious, or so I hoped, anyway."

Jeremy stopped and looked at me, as if to see if I believed him, then continued. "But now I was panicked, and I began running. I eventually stopped, saw the big spires, and knew our camp was in the opposite direction, and once I got out of the trees I finally found my way back. I'm not used to these altitudes, and I can tell you that my heart was pounding from both fear and exertion. And when I saw the chopper, I kind of followed it back to where it sounded like it had landed."

I made sure Jeremy got on the right airplane for his return trip to L.A., thankful he'd made it out OK. I wasn't sure how I would ever explain to the RCMP how an artist from one of my heli-trips was missing in the Bugaboos, and I was glad I wouldn't have to.

Jeremy had taken extra care to get his painting wrapped and shipped home, and I wondered what he would tell people about it.

Anyway, I soon sold the business, like I said earlier, and I had no remorse. I was glad to be back on my own schedule and able to spend my days painting instead of making sure clients were well taken care of on my heli-trips.

The one thing I didn't predict was my complete lack of interest in going back into the Bugaboos. I haven't been back, even though I've had a few friends ask if I'd guide them back in there to paint. For some reason, the thought of going back makes me feel really scared.

I just tell them. "There are things up there that will mess up your painting," and let it go at that.

8. The Face at Lost Lake Road

Once in awhile I hear a story that makes the hair on my neck stand up, and this is one. These kinds of stories usually have no logical explanation, at least not that I can think of.

This one really made me stop and think about things, especially my take on the natural world around us—it's not always how we perceive it, sometimes not even close.

This gal told us this story over lunch after Sarah and I met her skiing at Mt. Warner near our hometown of Steamboat Springs, Colorado. I will say that it's certainly different from anything I've ever heard before.

—Rusty

This incident happened when I was in my 30s, not all that many years ago, as I'm now 46, but it seems like forever. The stress was with me for a number of years, and that's probably why it seems so long ago.

Pain can make time move more slowly, it seems. Had I known what that little two-track road off the highway would hold for me, I would've just kept going.

I'd met a guy the previous summer in Sandpoint, Idaho, my hometown, where I was living and working. He was from Canada and just doing some hiking and sightseeing in the U.S. for a few weeks of vacation. He had a pickup and was pulling a little teardrop trailer.

We became friends, and he invited me to come visit him at his home in Penticton, British Columbia. So, when I had a few days off, I headed up there.

When I crossed the border at Nelway, they were less than friendly. Maybe it was my dreadlocks and general scruffy appearance, but it basically constituted harassment. They made me prove I had enough funds to spend a week in Canada.

I had this happen at the Mexican border in Nogales a few years before that, except they made me pay a small fee to enter the country (some would call it graft), and to their credit, at least the Canadians didn't do that.

But this plays into what happens, because on the way back, I decided to drive a little further east across Canada and go through a different border entry point.

If I'd just crossed again at Nelway going back, all this wouldn't have happened, so maybe I should send the border guards at Nelway a bill for the psychiatric services that resulted, since they'd started the whole thing by making me want to take a new route.

Anyway, I'd had a great week with my new friend, Kelly. We said our goodbyes and I headed out. I thought about crossing at the Midway crossing, as it was right there, but I'd been that way before, so I figured I might as well see some new country. So, I kept going east, staying on the Canadian side of the border. I decided I'd cross near Creston at the Porthill crossing, which is almost due north of Sandpoint.

For some reason, as I drove along through Canada, I felt a sense of consolation knowing my home country was only a few miles away, and there were several border crossings I'd be going by, should I decide to go south earlier.

I was kind of thinking I would be harassed again if I went through a small crossing like Nelway, so I voted for Porthill, which sees more traffic. My friend Kelly said the U.S. customs seemed generally more accepting of hippie types, but I was worried anyway.

So, I left Penticton and headed south, then east on the Crowsnest Highway, which goes east, then north, then south, then east, then north—you get the picture. It follows the border, making a jagged line on the map, due to the mountains and lakes in the region.

I got to Carson and almost crossed the border there, then changed my mind at the last minute and drove to the nearby town of Grand Forks instead. Going through Carson would make me have to drive back west again for awhile, and I wasn't real fond of making the trip longer.

Canada has this thing called Tim Hortons, sort of a Starbucks type business, but with better food. Every town of any size in Canada has a Tim Hortons. Starbucks is making its way into the country, so you'll sometimes see them, and Starbucks actually has better coffee, in my opinion.

By the time I reached Grand Forks, I was jonesing pretty bad for a cup of brew and hoping to see a Tim Hortons. Well, lo and behold, I couldn't believe my eyes, the town had an independent espresso drive-through. It was called Jitters, and the coffee was okay, but what I remember most was a sign that said, "B.C. Idle Free," telling you to shut off your engine when in line. Funny how things like that stick with you, and I can barely recall what the espresso place even looked like.

I was soon back on the road. It was B.C. Day, but I didn't know it at the time, and I couldn't figure out why all the traffic. I was soon at Christina Lake, and boy did I like that place. It was really pretty, a long lake set in the mountains with lots of sailboats and little cottages. I vowed to go back there someday for a vacation, but I haven't yet.

On I drove, until I came to the little town of Trail. I was within spitting distance of the border crossing at Waneta, but I was set on going through at Porthill, partly because it was a straight shot on down to Sandpoint.

I'm not really sure where it was, somewhere between Salmo and Creston, that I started up Kootenay Pass. By this time, I wanted to stop and take a break, and since I had my two labs with me, I wanted to let them out for a bit.

But I couldn't find any place to stop except along the highway. I wanted to let the dogs run for a bit, so I kept looking for a little side road or someplace where I could get away from the traffic.

All of a sudden, I saw a little break in the trees along the highway. I quickly stopped and turned off, and I could see a little two-track road coming out of the forest. I turned onto it, thinking I would pull off far enough to let the dogs out without being near traffic, take a quick break, then head on back down the highway.

There was an old rusted sign wired to a post, but I couldn't make out anything except the words, "Lost Lake." The weeds growing up in the middle of the little road rubbed the bottom of my car, and I figured I was on an old overgrown logging road. The road immediately dropped into a small draw, and I could tell from the thick willows and tall trees that it followed a stream.

After a few hundred feet, the road climbed up a steep hill, so I found a place to turn around in the grasses and stopped before the hill, letting the dogs out. I didn't want to get myself into a place where I couldn't turn around, and I had no idea where that steep hill went to.

The first thing the dogs did was find a little tributary coming off the stream and wade in, getting soaking wet. Being labs, they were pretty easy to please, and they were splashing, wagging their tails, taking big drinks and playing in the water. It was a peaceful little spot, just what we needed.

I walked around a bit, taking a few photos with my little pocket Nikon. The foliage was too thick to easily walk over to the stream itself, and it looked like there were wild roses growing everywhere, which means thorns, so I pretty much just walked along the little road a ways.

Part of me wanted to drive up that hill to see what I could see, but it was late afternoon, and I needed to get going. I turned around and started back towards the car when I saw it—a bear track, and a big one! And it looked really fresh!

I hadn't even considered there might be bears around, and I felt a surge of adrenaline. I called the dogs, tried to dry them off, then got them into the car. They were still wet, but I was more worried about a bear being nearby than my car getting a little wet and muddy.

I felt safe in the car, so I paused and looked all around, wondering if the bear was anywhere nearby. I would like to see it, but only from the safety of my car and if it were going the opposite direction.

I didn't notice anything, and it was time to go. Seeing that track had changed the entire feel of the place. It had initially seemed like a little idyllic piece of paradise, but now it felt more like an isolated danger zone where no one would find me if something happened. There wasn't even any cell service down in the draw. I hadn't thought much about pulling off down in there, with the highway no less than quarter mile away, as I knew I could always walk out and flag someone down if I had trouble.

I was ready to start the car when I suddenly felt exhausted, overwhelmed by grogginess. I needed a nap. I was so tired I could barely keep my eyes open.

I checked on the dogs. They were sound asleep in the back. I had the presence of mind to lock the car doors, but I don't remember anything after that.

When I woke, it was pitch black outside. I thought I could hear something like a lion roaring, like out of some nature movie about Africa, but it wasn't very close.

I couldn't believe it! I'd slept four hours. I'd stopped on trips before and taken little naps in the car, but usually for only 10 or 15 minutes, then I was refreshed enough to keep going. But four hours! Something was wrong.

I couldn't check my cell phone to see if its clock matched my car's, since there was no service, but I knew

I'd slept awhile, as it had only been mid-afternoon when I'd stopped there, and now it was dark.

I had trouble waking up, but something said I needed to get out of there. Looking into the back, I could see the dogs were still asleep. This was so unlike them, as they were both young and pretty hyper.

A sense of dread filled me, and I worried the car wouldn't start, but fortunately, it started right up. It was iffy trying to see the two-track to drive out, as it was hard enough to follow in the daylight, but I was soon at the highway.

I turned onto the blacktop and felt an immense sense of relief. I couldn't wait to get away from from Lost Lake Road. It sure wasn't a road well-traveled, or traveled at all, for that matter.

I drove on home, getting back during the night, and I've never been happier to crawl into my bed. All the way back, I would stop occasionally to take a break, and the dogs would not get out of the car. I stopped at a fast-food place in Bonner's Ferry and got them burgers, and they wouldn't touch them. This was totally unheard of for them.

I woke up late the next morning with a headache, the dogs going in and out of the dog door, seeming perfectly normal, finally eating the burgers. But I felt like I had a hangover and it didn't go away until that evening.

OK, I thought about this often, about why I slept so long, then I finally dismissed it as pretty much nothing. I'd had a good time with Kelly. We'd done a lot of hiking, and I'd been more tired than I thought. That was all.

Still, it was very unusual for me. First of all, I don't generally feel safe enough in my car to sleep like that, especially out in an unknown area. Second, for me to take a nap that long was unheard of. I thought maybe I was catching a bug, but I never got sick, but maybe I'd kicked it by sleeping so long.

I went back to work, and after a few days was back in my old routine—walk the dogs, go to work, come home, walk the dogs, eat dinner, do whatever, then go to bed.

Weekends I spent doing all the things I couldn't do the rest of the week—get groceries, do laundry, go to a movie or out to dinner, and go for a long hike with the dogs.

A month had passed, and I'd pretty much forgotten the whole incident on Lost Lake Road. Except I now felt something I'd never felt before—a longing to go back—and not just to Canada, but to that peaceful little two-track road. I guess I forgot how scared I'd been there.

With time, I actually began to yearn for it, and I think what happened is it became symbolic for me of a life without all the stress and worry that goes with having a hectic job in a city, though Sandpoint's not very big. The quiet and open country and pure air and big trees and babbling creek there along that road—it all took on a sort of mythic dimension, symbolizing a peaceful life, and I wanted to go back.

I even bought a map of B.C. and circled the spot and put it on my office wall. I've been to lots of pristine places, and living where I did, I wasn't that far from the backcountry. But none of these places ever had this effect on me.

Well, about six weeks after my innocent stop at Lost Lake Road, it started. I woke in the middle of the night in a cold sweat, and even with my eyes open, I could see a huge dark hairy face with a pushed-in nose and big eyes and big yellow teeth, staring at me through my window. Problem was, the blinds on my windows were closed and my bedroom was upstairs in my house.

When I recovered enough to realize where I was, I turned on the bedroom light. The dogs were fast asleep, and I realized it had to have been a dream—or more like a nightmare.

I wasn't able to go back to sleep, so I went downstairs and made myself a cup of coffee and waited for dawn, which wasn't that far off.

That face stuck with me all day. There'd been something so real and immediate about it that it was hard to believe it was a dream.

I was kind of hesitant to go to bed that night, still remembering the face, but I watched some late-night TV and soon forgot all about it.

That night was fine, but the night after, there it was— and the night after that. I moved into the guest bedroom, and it then looked at me through the bathroom window, which one can see from the bed. I closed the bathroom door, and now it was on the ceiling.

The face now followed me wherever I went. I couldn't get away from it. I even spent the weekend at a friend's house, and it followed me there.

This had been going on for weeks, and I was turning into a nervous wreck. I didn't want to go to sleep and would stay up until I couldn't help it, then doze off. I would find myself sleeping in the strangest places—sitting at the kitchen table, nodding off at my computer desk—and I was becoming more and more sleep deprived.

But through it all, my solace was that image I'd built in my mind of Lost Lake Road, and the thought of escaping everything and going there became a peaceful feeling I could invoke when the face became overwhelming. I had no clue that Lost Lake Road and the face could be related.

Finally, my boss asked me into his office for a meeting about my performance. Did I realize that I'd become a liability to the company? I was well-paid and producing almost nothing.

There was no way I could tell him what was going on, so I just mumbled something about having some stress-related problems. He told me the company would pay any therapy or psychiatric bills and asked me to start immediately. I had been a valued employee, and they didn't want to lose me.

Well, at this point, I had no choice, but I seriously doubted if anyone could help. I had no idea where this image came from.

So, I started seeing a psychiatrist. It took awhile and some courage to work up to the problem, but I finally told her what was going on.

She was sympathetic and said we needed to explore what the face represented, probably something I'd deeply repressed since my childhood. This could take some time. Was I committed to doing this therapy work? I said yes, even though something told me we weren't even vaguely on the right track.

But she'd prescribed sleeping pills, and I was finally able to sleep again. My work went right back up to where it had been, and my manager seemed satisfied that all was going well.

I saw the doctor every week, and we began to try to figure out what the face represented, but it felt like we were going nowhere.

After a few months of not seeing the face, I was beginning to think it was all over, until the night I decided to take up a friend on her offer to stay at her family cabin in the woods over by Flathead Lake. I had a three-day weekend, and it would soon be winter. This was my last chance to get out.

I knew the dogs would love it, and I could go spend a couple of days relaxing from my stressful job, just going for hikes and reading books. I really looked forward to it.

The cabin was everything I expected, except for the face. I saw it again the first night, and it was even more terrifying than before. My shrink had tried to figure out what it symbolized, but I couldn't think of anything, as I'd had a pretty good childhood. Now, here it was, back again.

I knew it wasn't symbolic of anything, but I couldn't figure it out. I was packing my things to leave the next morning, too afraid to even take the dogs out, when I sat down in shock.

Could it be? I finally made a connection—it dawned on me that the face had something to do with my long nap on Lost Lake Road. I knew I was right, because it felt like something was now close to being resolved.

This same face must have looked in at me while I was sleeping—had I somehow opened my eyes long enough to see it, but repressed it deep into the depths of my mind?

The shrink was right, it was something deep in my subconscious, but it wasn't symbolic of anything, it was real.

I shivered, loaded my stuff into my car, put the dogs in, locked the cabin, and headed out. But instead of going in the direction of home, I felt compelled to go north.

I was soon crossing the border, on my way back to Lost Lake Road. I knew I was in for a long drive, but it just felt like something I had to do if I ever wanted peace, resolution, and sleep.

I stopped in Creston for the night, closing in on my destination. I didn't want to be on the Lost Lake Road in the dark, so I had to time it just right.

By then, it was Saturday night. There was no way I could get to the lake and back to work in one day, but I didn't even think about it. I knew I had to go back and figure out what happened. My sanity depended on it.

I called my credit card company so they would know I was traveling and not shut my card down, as I had only a couple of hundred dollars in cash. I was on the road again early Sunday morning, and the dogs seemed happy to be going somewhere, and I would stop periodically to walk them.

Now that I was close to my destination, I was having serious second thoughts. Why was I going back? It was just a little spot on an old abandoned road, so why had it become such an epic place for me?

I crossed over Kootenay Pass and soon found the Lost Lake turnoff on the other side and stopped, sitting there by the highway for the longest time, seriously doubting my actions.

What did I expect to find? Why was I doing this? It was purely a compulsion.

Driving slow, I dropped down into the little draw, then turned around and stopped, just like before. It was a beautiful day, and the place looked just like it had—nothing special, but pretty enough. I had already decided that if I got sleepy, I would immediately leave. No more long naps.

I got out and looked around, remembering the grizzly track, but nothing looked amiss. I then called the dogs, but they refused to get out. They'd been out not long before, but it was still unlike them. They were always ready to run around.

I stretched and stood there, looking around. The place felt just like any other pretty valley, and that sense of peace and refuge wasn't there any more than any other place out in the woods.

This surprised me, as I'd even fantasized about building a little cabin there, and now it really didn't feel like anything special. I sighed. I'd driven like a mad woman for miles, burning money I didn't have to get there, and now I felt let down. Somehow, I'd thought that coming back would give me some kind of closure or some kind of new direction. I had even been researching immigrating to Canada.

And now, I felt nothing, just let down.

But as I leaned against the car, something made me do a double take. There, in the trees along the creek, no more than 30 feet away, was a shape in the shadows. I froze, suddenly scared, my hand on the car door handle, ready to jump in.

I was mesmerized for a moment, my eyes adapting to the shade. It was some kind of grizzly bear, I thought, given its size and shadowy shape. But now, seeing that I spotted it, it stepped out into the sunlight where I could see it perfectly, the exact opposite reaction of what I would expect.

It wasn't a bear—it was something human-like, though much larger, and it had brownish-yellow hair all over its body. It was massive, and as it turned to where I could see it better, I almost fainted.

It was the same face I'd been seeing in my dreams.

It made no motion to come closer, and I stood for what seemed like eternity, trying to process what I was seeing. How could this be? How could I be standing there seeing my dream, or rather, my nightmare? Was I asleep and thinking I was awake? What was it about this place that had driven me back to it and to this creature?

It had to be a Bigfoot, a Sasquatch. I knew my hunch was right—I had somehow seen it when I was taking my long nap. It must have leaned and looked into my car window, and I had somehow repressed the sight, relegating it to my dream world. My shrink wouldn't believe this, I thought.

And the longer I stood there looking at it, the less fearful I became. I finally asked, "Are you real?" As I asked the question, it slipped back into the thick brush and trees. It was gone, just like that, and it left a deep feeling of peace and contentment behind.

I got into my car and drove up the old logging road and was soon back on the highway. I stopped again down the road a little further, letting the dogs out, then headed home.

Once again, I arrived back in Sandpoint late at night. The dogs were really happy to be home, but as I crawled into bed, exhausted, I felt a bit of a longing to be back on the road to Lost Lake.

I can't explain it, but I still feel this way, years later. I never dreamed about or saw the face again, and I know that someday I'll go back. I feel that my fears have been conquered.

I hope to go and camp there someday. I now have no fear of the face, and my yearning for the place hasn't gone away, but I think it's more of a yearning for freedom in nature.

To me, it's embodied in that great creature, and I may or may not ever see it again, but I wish it well.

9. The Mount Robson Whisperer

I met this woman, who I'll call Linda, on a fly-fishing trip on the Big Hole River in Montana, where we'd had a couple of great campfire talks, including yarns by two guys who told Bigfoot stories so outlandish that they were totally unbelievable. (For example, how often does a Bigfoot come into your kitchen when you're at work and make you a berry pie, leaving you a note saying it's for dinner—that kind of thing). Their stories were fun, but ridiculed the whole idea that Bigfoot actually existed.

Linda sat there listening, and I could tell she was uncomfortable. I approached her later in private and asked if she'd been upset by the stories. She replied that she hadn't, but she knew Sasquatch was real. She was Canadian, and I knew she had something to say about the subject, more than I would ever guess as she told me her story.

Incidentally, she seemed like a very intelligent and sensitive woman, and I've always thought that such women were more likely to have Bigfoot encounters, as these creatures seem to intuit they'll be taken seriously and yet not be harmed.

—Rusty

I was born and raised in the city of Calgary, Alberta, and if you've ever been there, you'll know that the Canadian Rockies are a bit of a distance from the city (about an hour's travel), yet still form a strong presence. They stand on the western horizon, and if you were a kid who had a bit of adventure in your blood, you'll understand the draw they had on me, even from that many kilometers.

We lived on a bit of a rise, and I recall looking out my upstairs bedroom window for hours with binoculars, studying the distant jagged skyline, trying to correlate the points with a map I'd gotten from somewhere. They seemed so far away and intriguing.

Of course, like everyone in the city, we'd go to the mountains for holidays, including Christmas in Banff, which my mom loved. It was always snowy there for the season's festivities, and I recall being totally enchanted with being right smack in the middle of the same mountains I could see on the far horizon from my bedroom window.

But other than that, and an occasional picnic in the high country, we didn't spend much time there. Everyone was too busy, and it was hard to get away.

As I got older, I started reading about the early explorers and the history of the region, then transitioned to reading about the big peaks themselves and the climbers. It seemed rather surreal and distant to me. I remember my cousin, Casey, visiting one time and telling me I was destined to be a mountaineer. I think I was about 12, and he really helped plant the seed.

Well, I was now in college at the University of Alberta and had yet to climb a single peak. I had no car, so no way to get to the mountains to climb. They still felt intimidating and intriguing to me, and I must say, given the nature of the Rockies, they are exactly that. Once I graduated, I went on to grad school in Quebec, living there for six years, far from my beloved Rockies.

But the big peaks always pulled me back, and I couldn't wait to return to Alberta after I graduated. With a newly-minted PhD, I was lucky and got a good job with my alma mater, the University of Alberta, teaching history. I'd written my thesis on the history of the Canadian Rockies, so all my youthful interest and studies had helped me there.

I was elated to be back, and even more elated to find there was a group of students who had started a mountaineering club. Even though I was now an assistant professor, I started attending, and I was soon on my first outing with the group, most of them much younger than I was and much more experienced.

I don't even recall where we went, but I do remember how excited I was to finally be living my so-called destiny, even though I really believe we make our own destinies by following our interests.

Well, enough of the philosophizing, let's just say I was like a little kid, one who had studied everything she could get her hands on and was finally getting to go see the big peaks in person.

But there was one thing I hadn't studied, even with all the years of background reading since I was young—one thing I didn't even dream existed, yet alone could live in my beloved mountains. And that one thing has left an indelible mark on my so-called destiny as a mountaineer—it stopped me dead in my tracks.

Let me explain. I'd now been a professor for several years and had graduated from the mountaineering club into a group of like-minded souls who were more my peers age-wise, local climbers and mountaineers who were serious about their so-called hobby.

With the encouragement and help of this group, I'd climbed a number of peaks, including my favorite of all, Mount Edith Cavell, named for a Canadian nurse who was killed by the Nazis. I had quickly become a seasoned climber, and everyone told me I was a natural. Most of our expeditions weren't technical, though there were a few places where we had to have some technical skills and equipment. We were more mountaineers, not technical climbers.

I don't think a person could climb all the peaks in Alberta in their lifetime, yet alone those in nearby B.C., but I'd been inspired by a climber who'd given a talk at the university about summiting the Big Seven, the highest peak on each of the world's seven continents, including Mount Everest.

He'd encouraged everyone to set some mountaineering goals, and I decided that, since I wasn't much of a technical climber, I wanted instead to do a photo project of the 10 highest peaks in the Canadian Rockies, maybe even turn it into a coffee-table book. I wasn't a good enough climber to actually summit them all, though I knew I could make it up a few. By then, I'd bought myself a nice camera and was really getting into photography.

Of course, Mount Robson was right up there at the top, being the tallest peak in the Canadian Rockies and also having the greatest prominence, or rise from base to top. But Robson has the nickname of "the Great White Fright" for a reason. It's nearly unclimbable, and not climbable at all by the average climber or even by many good climbers.

For example, the Kain Face, which was the first climbed route, takes three to four days, and Conrad Kain, the first to summit it, chopped 700 steps in the ice to get to the top. I knew there was no way I could ever climb it, but I wanted to go see as much of it as I could.

I guess I should stop here and say that I'm giving you all this backstory so you won't think I'm crazy when you hear what I'm about to tell you. You may think I'm crazy anyway, and maybe I am, but I do lead a pretty normal life.

But everyone has a hobby or interest—some do art, some like music, some live to garden, and mine was going into the mountains. I guess I like a challenge, plus being out in nature, and there's truly no place more beautiful than the Canadian Rockies. Adding photography to the mix seemed really cool to me.

So here I was, obsessed with photographing Mount Robson, especially the waterfalls on the back side of the mountain, where one can see the glaciers calving into Berg Lake, if you're lucky.

I wanted to hike up the Berg Lake Trail and into the Valley of a Thousand Falls. It's considered to be one of the most amazing hikes in the world, as the trail takes you to the backside of the peak and right under the Mist and Berg glaciers, which, along with Hargreaves Glacier, feed the numerous incredible waterfalls that have been likened to those in Yosemite.

The Berg Lake Trail is a world-renowned backcountry hiking trail. It's about 12 miles to the lake with an elevation gain of about 2,600 feet and a totally crazy hike to try in one day, except for the fact that you're allowed to mountain bike the first four miles, as the trail follows an old road.

Lots of people rent mountain bikes and do this first part on wheels. This makes the actual hike a little shorter, but it's still a totally crazy distance. But a number of people do it in one long day, partly because the campgrounds up by the lake are usually full, reserved far in advance, so they have no choice if they want to see the falls and glaciers.

I decided I would go spend a weekend scoping it all out. Since I didn't have a reservation for any of the camp-grounds, I decided to just sleep at the visitor lodge parking lot in my van, then get as far up the trail as I could and turn back, making it a long day hike. If I got up early enough, I was confident I could get to Berg Lake.

It was, of course, summer, and I was teaching only one class, so I had weekends free from grading homework, which I seem to do endlessly during the regular school year and which slows me way down on getting out.

I was so excited. I got all my gear ready and headed out. It's not a real close drive from Calgary to Mount Robson Provincial Park, but driving up the amazing Icefields Park-way makes the drive seem shorter.

So, I got into Jasper late Friday evening, stopped for dinner, then drove to the park, which was about an hour's drive. It was a beautiful full moon night in July, and I'll never forget the ethereal feeling of driving from Jasper to Mount Robson. It felt otherworldly.

I was soon to find out it was indeed an otherworldly place, nothing like I was expecting. But I'm getting ahead of myself here.

It was about 9 p.m. when my headlights lit up the big white mountain goat on the sign that reads, "Mount Robson Provincial Park." I decided to stop right there and camp in the parking lot by the picnic area, still a ways from the visitor headquarters.

There was no one around, and I was exhausted. I slept like a baby in my van until about 2 a.m., when I needed to get up to pee. I was startled by what looked like a giant white ghost in front of my vehicle, then realized it was the big goat on the sign, the full moon lighting it up.

I crawled back into bed, but after that, I slept fitfully. I never could get back to a deep sleep, but kept imagining someone was talking to me, kind of in a low voice, telling me I should go home.

It sounded a bit like my Uncle Ed, who I'd been close to and had passed away about a year earlier. It was eerie. Around 5 a.m. I finally got up, turned on a light, and made a cup of tea.

As I sat there drinking it, I felt compelled to turn the light back off, as if someone were looking in at me. I checked the door locks, then crawled back into bed and put my head under the covers. I would calm myself down, then get up and head out. I needed to get an early start if I wanted to make it to Berg Lake.

Instead of getting up, I went back to sleep, though I hadn't intended to. When I woke, it was around eight in the morning and people were coming and going, stopping right next to my van to have their pictures taken by the sign.

I couldn't believe I'd slept that late, and I was irritated at myself, because it meant a late start on the trail, which was still a ways away, down by the visitor center.

After a quick breakfast, I drove on, wondering why the night had seemed so strange. Had I really heard my uncle's voice telling me to turn back? I'm not at all superstitious and actually don't even believe in ghosts, but it made me feel uncertain, and I almost did turn back. I wish now that I had.

I was soon at the visitor center, then drove up the road to the trailhead for Berg Lake. I was surprised at the lack of cars, as usually it's really hard to find a place to park there. There's a very short window when one can hike in the Canadian Rockies due to the endless winter there, so these kinds of hikes are often totally overwhelmed with people in the summer. I think it was just a fluke that the trail wasn't crowded with people that day.

It didn't take me long to get the four or so miles to Kinney Lake, as the trail is really easy and I was hiking really fast, trying to make up for the lost time when I'd been sleeping. I noted that the campground looked partly empty, and I didn't see many people around, though I had passed a few on the trail.

I crossed the wobbly suspension bridge that leads into the Valley of a Thousand Falls and was soon to Whitehorn

Campground, another three miles on up the trail from Kinney Lake. I wasn't even winded, and I was proud of myself for making such good time. I thought that I might be able to get to the lake after all, in spite of my late start.

After passing Kinney Lake, the few hikers and bikers I had seen must have turned back, as I soon found myself hiking in solitude.

I was soon to the base of Whitehorn Hill, where I was absolutely mesmerized by the beauty surrounding me, the immense peaks and glaciated landscape. I felt like I had the most beautiful place in all the Canadian Rockies to myself, the ultimate of all the fantasies I'd had as a kid. I didn't know it, but what was yet to come was even more fantastic, in the true sense of the word.

The trail now began to climb, gaining elevation quickly, slowing me down. I gained over 1300 feet in two miles, all the while catching glimpses of thundering falls through the trees—White Falls, Falls of the Pool, and finally, Emperor Falls. I'd seen photos of Emperor Falls and decided to take a quick sidetrack and follow a short spur to its base.

Emperor Falls is absolutely amazing, a wide falls that one can stand almost directly under, if they like being pelted with small chunks of ice. I stayed longer than I should have there, taking photos of the falls with Mount Robson in the background. I felt that if I got no farther than that, it would still be an amazing day.

As I finally gathered my photo gear and left the falls, I stopped and turned back for a moment to take one last photo, and what I saw really puzzled me. There, almost under the falls, exactly where I'd been standing, was a dark figure that contrasted with the ice-white falls.

I wondered how I'd missed seeing someone else up there. As I watched, it seemed like the figure saw me looking back and quickly ducked down beside the trail where I couldn't see it. It all seemed very odd and gave me pause.

I now reached a stretch of brutally steep trail, and I recall thinking I should turn back. I was beginning to feel the stinging of lactic acid in my legs, a sign that your muscles need more oxygen. But I couldn't stop—I was so close to my destination, Berg Lake, and the glorious glaciers that hung right down almost into the lake itself. Maybe I'd get lucky and get a photo of one of the glaciers calving a big chunk into the lake.

I finally reached the end of the steep climb and the site of Emperor Falls Campground, which was filled with tents, but not many people. I figured they were all out climbing or hiking.

I'd now come 10 miles and was very tired. It was time for a break. I sat down on a big rock and drank lots of water, eating the sandwiches I'd brought, along with some high-protein snack bars. I chased it all down with some apple slices and peanut butter, kind of amazed at how much I was eating. But I knew I needed the energy to get back down. I wasn't out of the woods yet, so to speak.

I suddenly felt disappointed and demoralized. In retrospect, I knew all along it would be a long and difficult hike, but the reality of it hit me then and there. I'd stopped too long and lost my momentum.

I still had almost two miles until I could actually see Berg Lake itself, and it was even farther to get around the lake far enough to really see Mist and Berg glaciers. And it was now early afternoon. I'd made really good time, but I knew I would be closing in on my physical limitations just to hike back out the distance I'd come, not to mention if I decided to carry on a few more miles.

Well, being me, I just stood up and continued. I had no idea when I'd be back up there, and I'd be darned if I weren't going to get some photos of the glaciers and the Emperor Face of Mount Robson, the summit rising 8,000 feet from the lake. I knew I was in epic country, and I had practically killed myself to get there, and there was no way I was going to give up until I saw what I'd come to see.

I hiked along a flat alluvial plain for another couple of miles until I finally reached Marmot Campground and the first views of the lake. I'd managed to get my second wind and felt better. Another mile and I was at Berg Campground.

I knew I needed to hike yet one more mile to get to the best views of the glaciers, but I just didn't have it in me. I was beginning to wonder if I could even make it all the way back, even though it was all downhill.

Well, I decided to stop there, mostly because I couldn't continue. I actually had incredible views of the glaciers, and I could hear them calving. It was an incredible sound, the grinding and crushing of ice. The blue-green waters of Berg Lake made a stunning foreground to Mount Robson, which towered above it all, its very top hid in a cloud. It was an unearthly and indescribable scene of power and beauty.

I then realized why I'd always been so attracted to these massive mountains, ever since I could remember. They inspired me, made me feel like there was more to life than mundane everyday stuff, and I knew that, no matter how despairing or difficult life might get, these places of supreme beauty were out there, holding the planet together. Such places made me happy, even if I wasn't able to be out in them. Just thinking of them was enough to ground me.

I don't know how long I was there, just soaking it all in and trying to capture it in photos, but I finally realized I needed to get back. It seemed like a number of people had hiked past me, either going back to the trailhead or their camps, and I had pushed my limits, both physically and time wise.

I put my camera gear away, ate some gorp, and headed back down the trail, tired but happy.

I was easily back down to Emperor Falls, a new burst of energy propelling me along. I thought again of the figure I'd seen and wondered about it, then decided it had to have been someone hiding in the rocks while I was there. Still, it felt kind of odd, and when I passed the spur to the falls I began feeling a sense of foreboding. I picked up my pace, knowing I was now in a race with the daylight to make it out.

I tramped through the Valley of a Thousand Falls, now feeling fatigued and hardly even noticing the stunning waterfalls all around me. It was now late afternoon, and there seemed to be no one else on the trail. Everyone had probably camped or were ahead of me, I figured.

I finally reached the swinging bridge and hardly remember crossing it, whereas the first time across, its swinging had unsettled me. Now, I was so exhausted I hardly even knew where I was. I stopped for a moment and ate a handful of nuts and drank some water. I was seriously wondering if I would make it back out at all, yet alone before dark.

I had let my compulsive nature get the best of me, something any serious mountaineer knows can mean trouble—or worse, possible death. It's critical to always be aware of where one is in the grand scheme of things—how long it will take to get back, what the weather's doing, one's mental and physical condition, etc. Failing to maintain a high level of awareness can lead to trouble, something I knew from reading about all the mountaineering disasters.

I knew this well, and even as I walked along, I was aware on a certain level that I was becoming seriously tired, but I couldn't figure out why. I had taken the time to re-energize, eating and drinking frequently, and I was in great shape. Even though it was a long strenuous hike, I shouldn't have felt so out of it.

My brain felt kind of fuzzy, and I wasn't thinking as clearly as I normally would. I've been hypothermic, and your brain doesn't have enough energy to think clearly, as you're kind of in a haze and can do stupid things. But I know I wasn't hypothermic up there on the trail under Mount Robson. For some reason, I just wasn't thinking clearly.

I've discussed this with a couple of close friends, and maybe it was from not sleeping well the previous night, but yet it didn't feel like sleep deprivation. It's just hard to explain. I could now again hear my uncle's voice in my mind, telling me I should go home.

I was on past Kinney Lake and was nearing the homestretch of the last four miles when I clearly heard someone whispering to me in a husky voice. At first I thought I was imagining my uncle again.

It was really strange, as it came from the shadows and was really loud, yet still a whisper. I knew then it was real, and not my imagination.

It sounded like someone said, "Let's take a break."

I stopped and turned all around, looking to see who was there. I suddenly felt the urge to flee, to run as fast as I could, but I managed to control myself, though I picked up the pace and started walking fast, like a power walker.

I was now making good time, especially considering how tired I was, but the shadows were quickly lengthening. I hadn't factored in the mountain blocking the sun, making it get dark earlier on the back side.

I stopped and felt in my day pack, getting out my headlamp. I wanted it handy, as it now felt like it was the only thing between me and getting lost in the dark. I then started power walking again. As I went by a particularly thick section of large trees and ferns, I heard someone whisper, "Let's have lunch."

In retrospect, it's kind of funny, the things I heard out there, but let me tell you that at the time, it was terrifying. I again felt the urge to run, and now I could feel the hair on the back of my neck and arms standing up. I also felt a sudden chill.

There was something out there, and it had to be very large to be able to "whisper" at a volume that was more like someone talking in a loud voice. All I could do was keep moving.

I now started to jog, even though I didn't want to trigger any predatory response by running, if whatever was weirding me out was indeed a predator of some kind.

But I was quickly winded. I stopped and again took off my pack, getting out my bear spray. It then dawned on me how totally out of it and careless I'd been. I would normally carry my bear spray on my belt where I could quickly reach it, not in my pack where it would do me no good if I were to meet a bear.

And as aware as I was of my fuzzy thinking, I couldn't muster myself into a normal state. It was almost as if I'd been drugged. And as I stood there, fiddling with my bear spray, hooking it to my belt, I heard the voice again, now coming from a shadowy draw a bit below the trail.

"Time to turn back," it whispered.

The whisperer was clearly messing with my mind, but there was nothing I could do but keep going. I was beginning to think I was hallucinating the whole thing.

I now recognized a landmark rock and felt a sense of hope. It was almost dark, and my heart was thumping in my chest so hard I was worried I'd have a heart attack. I walked for awhile, then started jogging again, trying to not actually run, for I knew I would quickly get winded and have to stop.

After awhile, I started getting a catch in my side, so I slowed down. And again, the voice whispered out, "Looks like rain."

What the heck? Whatever it was, real or not, it made no sense. Then suddenly a lightbulb lit up in my mind. This thing was repeating things it had heard hikers say on the trail. Whatever or whoever it was, it was trying to make me think it was a human.

I shivered, then turned on my headlamp, the trail now dark enough I was beginning to have trouble making out rocks and twigs. The last thing I wanted to do was trip and fall. I knew the full moon would rise not long after dark, but I hoped to be long gone by then.

What was this thing doing? It was obviously following me out, but why? And what did it hope to accomplish with the whispering?

I knew the parking lot had to be close, as I recognized a small clearing I'd come through shortly after starting the hike.

And just then, I heard something coming down the trail behind me, something really noisy, breaking branches I had carefully stepped over.

I panicked and ran.

Now seeing the glint of my van in the moonlight, I sprinted the last 100 yards, my lungs on fire. Behind me I could hear something grunting and stomping as if trying to catch me.

I quickly unlocked the door and jumped in, just as a large branch lobbed against the side of my van. For a brief second, I was terrified the van wouldn't start, but it did, and as I turned on the lights, I saw something black slip into the shadows.

I didn't see enough of it to tell what it was, except I did see some very powerful large shoulders slip into a thicket and disappear, a large conical head bent forward. Other then it having black fur or hair, that's all I saw, but I immediately thought of the figure at Emperor Falls.

I drove as fast as possible down the road and back to the highway, looking in my rearview mirror to see if it was following me, even though I knew I wouldn't be able to see it in the dark even if it were.

And as I drove along, my mind cleared, and I was able to think again. I drove all the way back to Jasper, where I stopped and parked along a street in a residential area, wanting to be surrounded by the comfort and security of town. I didn't care if the police ticketed me, but no one seemed to notice.

I was awake early the next morning, and it all still seemed surreal. After going to Tim Hortons for a coffee and donut, I was soon on my way home. When I arrived that afternoon, I simply went inside and collapsed, soaking in the security of being indoors, safe. I was totally traumatized.

I finally told a couple of good friends what had happened, and they were sure I'd seen a Sasquatch. I'd hardly even heard of such a thing, and I really didn't understand the whispering thing, but one friend said it must've been copying things hikers say, things it heard over and over on the trail.

I guess that makes some sense, though why it would do so, I don't know. Was it trying to fool me into thinking it was another hiker, then catch me off-guard? Was it intending to harm me? I don't know, but I'm sure never going back to see. I'm also now wondering if what I took as being my uncle wasn't another Sasquatch.

I've lost all interest in being in the mountains—in fact, I feel a sense of trouble when I think about going back. I guess maybe it's time for a change.

I spent a lot of my life obsessing over the Canadian Rockies, and now I'm beginning to get interested in other things. I love fly-fishing in the summer, and I'm thinking of taking up hockey in the winter.

But whatever I do, it won't be anywhere near Mount Robson.

10. Sasquatch Skedaddle

I heard this story over a campfire next to one of my favorite rivers, the Williams Fork, in Northwest Colorado, close to my home base. To me, it shows that Sasquatch has been a part of Canadian history for a long time, not even considering all the earlier native stories about these creatures.

It's an interesting twist that this event probably resulted in these settlers moving on to better and safer climes, and therefore the Sasquatch inadvertently saving their lives. And I can say I really have a lot of respect for these early people, as they had to be tough to survive—and so did the Squatches.

—Rusty

I'm going to tell you a story that came down in my family through, let's see, my dad, his dad, and his dad—including me, that makes four generations. This happened to my great-grandparents.

This happened in 1910, and my great-grandparents were both in their early 30s. It was just before my grandpa was born.

Anyway, my great-grandparents, Robert and Rebecca O'Riley, were some of the early pioneers in British Columbia. They came west from Ireland via Quebec, then made their way through the Canadian prairie provinces and on through Calgary, what there was of it, then on into the Okanagan Valley, a very good place for growing fruit and produce. It's actually called Canada's banana belt, and the fact that the climate is more moderate there than in most of Canada is probably the only reason they survived their first hard years.

Fruit orchards are the major crop in the Okanagan Country, which stretches clear down into the United States. Wine grapes are now a big crop, but I'm sure my great-grandparents would've been shocked to see that. They were tee-totalers and wouldn't touch alcohol in any form. That's a tradition that died out in my family, fortunately, and we all now enjoy a good glass of wine. Heck, we actually have a winery and make our own.

Where they lived became part of what's called the Fruit Highway. They eventually settled in a little town called Summerland, over on the west side of Okanagan Lake, but I was told this event happened over by Cherryville, further east and in the foothills of the Monashee Mountains. How they ended up in B.C. in the first place is unknown to me.

They were in their first year of homesteading a place, and it had been a hard go. (And by the way, one can still homestead in some parts of Canada, like Alberta.) My great-grandparents had barely grown enough food to make it through their first winter—mostly canned berries and some root foods like potatoes. Most of their food stuff was stored in a root cellar on their farm. Like most settlers, their main food supply was wild meat, like venison, which they dried and smoked and then hung in the root cellar or canned.

They lived in a small cabin, and the cellar was next door, half-buried in the ground with some rough stairs going down into it. These old root cellars did a good job of storing things, as being mostly underground, they moderated the temperatures to where things were kept cool but not freezing. Things like apples would store perfectly all winter.

British Columbia can have some brutal winters, but the Okanagan is known for being less severe, even somewhat moderate. But back in the early 1900s things were still very cold, even in the Okanagan. Scientists say the Little Ice Age ended pretty much in 1850, but the climate was still very severe in much of the north for some time after that.

Apparently my great-grandma kept a journal, and the year this happened, in 1910, she talked about day after day of subzero weather and snow so deep they had to dig tunnels five or six feet deep to get from the house to the cellar and the barn. This story is all from my great-grandmother's journal.

Fortunately, they had only two horses to feed, as a lot of farmers lost their stock that year from the severe blizzards. This was the same year of the Rogers Pass avalanche (in the Selkirk Mountains of B.C.), which killed 62 train workers, as well as the avalanche at Stevens Pass in Washington, which killed 96.

According to my great-grandmother's diary, winter hit hard and fast that year, with barely an autumn to speak of. She wrote of how happy she was that my great-grandpa had managed to shoot an extra deer that year, one more than they'd had the previous winter, which had been a touch-and-go season from a survival standpoint.

She had also learned to make pemmican from a local native, which is a high-energy mixture of meat and fat
and berries. It was a staple of natives and trappers, though
most of them were gone from that area by then.

Pemmican is made by cutting the leanest portions of
meat into thin strips and then drying it over a fire. After
it's dried, it's pounded into a powder, then melted together
with fat and berries and made into balls, which are then
stored, usually in leather bags.

Pemmican is famous for keeping well, supposedly even
for decades, and can be eaten as-is or fried. It's a very high-
energy food, and a couple of backpacking food companies
make energy bars that are pretty close to pemmican. Tanka
Bars and EPIC bars are some examples.

Anyway, pemmican was responsible for me being
around today to tell this story, as my great-grandmother
had made and stored a good amount of it in the back bedroom of their cabin, hanging it from the rafters. After the
incident I'm about to relate, it was all the food they had left,
but enough to get them out of there.

I've thought about this story a lot, and it seems to me
that what happened probably actually saved their lives, as
it forced them to leave before winter got too severe and the
snows were so deep they couldn't leave and would be stuck
there. It was a harsh winter, a winter many didn't survive.
But I'm getting ahead of myself.

Like I said, winter hit hard and fast. There wasn't much
to do each day, well, except keep the fire going, which
meant gathering wood, and it wasn't long before they
needed snowshoes to even get around, although they had

a big supply they'd gathered over the summer. And did I mention getting water from the nearby stream?

Also, there was feeding the horses, putting them out so they could get water from the stream (they had to be kept in the barn at night because of wolves), and all the other things that go with trying to survive in winter in British Columbia in what was probably a not-very-well insulated cabin.

It was a harsh life, but at least there weren't any brown bears around to worry about, as they had the sense to hibernate.

I'm just going to start calling them Grams and Gramps, OK? It's too hard to say all that "greats" stuff.

Well, once night, they heard a strange moaning coming from the direction of the barn. Gramps was worried it was wolves trying to get in to where the horses were, but Grams said no, it couldn't be wolves. It didn't sound anything at all like wolves to her.

They lay there in bed, speculating as to what it could be, when Gramps finally decided to go check it out. Grams was worried it was some of the native people come to steal their food or horses, but Gramps said that was ridiculous, as they sure as heck wouldn't be moaning and waking everyone up.

Now, lots of folks back then were very superstitious, as they didn't have the knowledge to explain things like we do now, so they just winged it. So, Grams decided it had to be some kind of spirit and forbade Gramps from leaving the cabin. Probably a good thing, considering what they found the next morning.

Something had tried to get into the cellar. There were big scratch marks all up and down the door, and Gramps found what looked like very large footprints, but they were pretty indistinct due to the fact that it had snowed some more during the night, partly covering them.

This was a puzzler, as the tracks were big, like a brown bear would leave, but it was far too cold for bears to be awake. Gramps figured it was a bear whose hibernation instincts had gone haywire, but Grams was suspecting one of the natives.

The problem with her theory is that most of the natives had migrated out of the mountains and into the milder coastal regions for the winter. Besides, the few who were around knew Grams would feed them if needed. Why bother to try to steal food when it could be freely obtained? Besides, she was a friend, as she always helped anyone in need.

OK, the next night, they heard the same moaning sound, but this time, dawn showed the root cellar had been broken into, and whoever did it had hands, because the door had been levered open, and on top of that, about a third of the canning jars had their lids wrenched off and were empty.

Someone had stolen lots of canned fruits and meats, as well as canned potatoes and beans and even some peppers. And whoever it was, they were barefoot and had huge feet, according to the tracks left in the snow.

Now Grams and Gramps were very upset. It had to be one of the natives, or possibly one of the crusty miners that made up most of the population of what was Cherryville at the time. But why remove the food from the jars and not just steal the jars themselves? Maybe they were carrying the food in some kind of packs, is what Gramps thought, but Grams said that didn't make sense, especially since it would all be mushed together.

Gramps had no idea what to do at this point. All their winter supplies—except the horses' hay and the pemmican in the cabin—were in that root cellar. They would die if any more of their food were stolen—in fact, just losing what they had so far now made getting through the winter an iffy proposition, even with the pemmican.

Gramps decided he would have to stand guard over the root cellar and catch whoever was stealing their food. There was no other way, as they couldn't risk losing any more supplies. But it was just too darn cold to hang around outside all night, hoping he would catch the thief. And what then? There was no court of law or anything he could do with whoever it was, just warn them off.

Gramps was a pretty inventive guy, and what he did was chisel out enough chinking in the cabin wall that he could see outside, right to the root cellar. Then, during the day, they could stuff a gunny sack in it to keep the cold out. It was a peep hole, and Gramps set himself up all comfortable where he could see out and began his vigil that very night. He also put an old board across the root cellar door, nailing it in place as an extra deterrent on top of the latch.

The cellar still held lots of canned goods, as well as the dried meat of two large deer and a beef Gramps had traded a fellow who wanted some wooden tools Gramps had carved.

Gramps dutifully sat there all night, but finally, in the early hours of the morning, his vision was blocked by snow. Another blizzard had come in, and it was a total whiteout.

Before winter had hit, Gramps had tied several ropes together and hung them from posts in the ground to guide him out to the barn to feed the horses, a sort of rope fence going from the barn to the house. He'd done this after hearing a neighbor had frozen to death the previous winter a mere 20 feet from his house in a blizzard, not realizing where he was.

Gramps went out and fed the horses, worried about them getting lost in the blizzard, so he kept them in. Surely it would clear off before long, and he could let them out for a drink of water. He hadn't made a rope path to the root cellar, just the barn, so he didn't go out that day to check things out, as they had food in the cabin.

The blizzard finally lifted that late afternoon and he was able to water the horses, then put them right back into the barn. by evening, the sky had cleared and it was bitter cold, the frozen snow crackling under his feet.

He finally managed to dig a path to the root cellar in the fresh snow, and what he then saw made his hair stand on end. The door had been completely lifted off its hinges and thrown a good 20 feet into a snowbank.

Looking inside, he could see that the place had literally been cleaned out. Everything was gone except broken glass jars, and even the venison and beef that had been hanging from the rafters was gone. Whoever had taken the food had to be very strong, or else they'd made a number of trips, and all during a raging blizzard!

He stumbled back inside the cabin, speechless. Finally, Grams went out to look for herself, and when she returned, she was also speechless. They both felt that they'd just received a death sentence, and the logistics of it seemed impossible. How could someone make off with so much food, and in a raging blizzard, no less? And who was strong enough to actually lift a heavy wooden door off its hinges and throw it that far?

They tried to sleep that night, but all they could do was talk about what it could be, and they both knew the answer—Sasquatch. Only a Sasquatch could do something like that, and hadn't there been plenty of talk about them ever since they'd come into this country? They'd been warned off by the natives, but they'd laughed, thinking it was just a legend.

I believe, from the stories I've heard, that Sasquatch was once much more plentiful in Canada, at least that part of the country, in the Okanagan Valley and Monashee Mountains. The native peoples seemed to have made a sort of truce with them, and they even revered them. But the white settlers began the big push to civilize everything, and it's my opinion that the Sasquatch moved to the more remote areas. That's just my thoughts on it.

Well, the next day, Grams and Gramps hitched up the horses to the wagon after putting on the sleigh rails, loaded up enough hay to feed the horses until they could get to the next settlement, added whatever they could fit of their personal things, and along with all that pemmican, headed out.

According to Grams' journal, the going was rough. The snow was deep, and the horses really struggled, and she and Gramps ended up walking most of the way, their feet wet and cold.

Their first night out, they slept under the wagon on a big moose pelt that kept out the snow. Grams wrote that they heard the same howling they'd heard at the cabin, but Gramps immediately shot off a couple of rounds from his rifle, and the creature left them alone. They were deathly afraid of it stealing their pemmican or even the horses.

They eventually made it to some settlement, I'm not sure where it was, but they spent the rest of the winter in a shared cabin with a couple of miners there. They ate on that pemmican the rest of the winter, and Gramps was able to trade some of it for some flour and sugar and that kind of thing.

The next spring, they moved further into the valley, where they settled in the small settlement of Summerland. They eventually somehow acquired a piece of land where they started an orchard and built a house, far from the mountains where the Sasquatch roamed.

My family managed to hold on to the property they'd settled, and it's now owned by my brother and I. We have a beautiful vineyard and winery there along what's called "Bottleneck Drive," a system of roads that connect the wineries. The land here is very fertile, and we grow some of the world's most flavorful grapes.

So, I really do believe that I wouldn't be here today if it weren't for a Sasquatch who forced my great-grandparents to move to a more habitable area. We feel very fortunate to live where we do, in one of the world's most beautiful places. We've worked hard here on this wonderful land they left us.

So, in honor of that Sasquatch who saved my great-grandparents' lives, we decided to make a very tasty red wine called, "Sasquatch Skedaddle." It's aged quite well and is full-bodied and robust, just like a Sasquatch.

Come by sometime and I'll pour you a glass.

11. The Bella Coola Hunter

*I first met Griz when I picked him up for a fishing trip at the air-
port in Hayden, Colorado, which services the town of Steamboat
Springs, my home base. Griz was an older guy, but he out-hiked
and out-fished us relatively younger guys, and I could tell he was
a seasoned outdoorsman.*

*Of course, when I found out where he was from, I understood,
as the Coastal Mountains of British Columbia are some of the
most rugged in the world—and the most beautiful, I might add.*

*Griz invited Sarah and I to visit his home town, and he
promised that if we did, he'd take me out Bigfooting (or Sas-
quatching, as he called it). I was excited, and Sarah and I talked
a lot about taking him up on his offer, which I hope to do someday, especially after hearing his story.*

—Rusty

I don't know if you've ever heard of the valley of Bella
Coola or not, but it's a very unique place. It's in the Coastal
Mountains of British Columbia, and even though it's technically not on the coast itself, the coast isn't far. Various
ferries shuttle people from Bella Coola to places like Vancouver.

Bella Coola's near the water, and the mountains tower above it, with glaciers and waterfalls galore. If you want to drive out of the valley, you have to go up what we call "the Hill," a road with an 18 percent grade that will take you up on the Chilcotin Plateau and eventually to Williams Lake, the nearest town of any size.

I actually live in the small village of Hagensborg, near the town of Bella Coola, and if you know Hagensborg, you can guess that I'm of Norwegian stock, straight from the original settlers, as the town's mostly made up of Norwegians and natives (the Nuxalk).

Everyone calls me "Griz" because I used to hunt grizzly bears. It was my claim to fame. I finally came to my senses after a good mauling, which was probably karma, if you believe in such. I almost lost my arm, and I have some pretty good scars. I still have a couple of big bear pelts, and I now feel bad that I killed these beautiful animals, even though one of their kind eventually tried to kill me.

Bears are smart and really don't want anything to do with humans in general. We see them all the time in the valley, even on the streets of Bella Coola and Hagensborg, and they generally leave everyone alone.

These bears are actually brown bears and are less aggressive than the interior grizzly bears as they have more food here on the coast—lots of salmon. So the word "grizzly" sometimes refers to the more aggressive interior brown bear, though they're basically the same species. But I just call them all grizzlies.

If you've ever watched the live bear cams at Katmai National Park in Alaska, you can see how big these brown bears are—they get huge. Anyway, there's a lot to the story about the grizzly mauling me, but I don't usually tell it all. But here goes—hold onto your hats!

There's something really primitive about hunting. I think it's maybe part of our DNA—well, men's DNA, anyway, from back when we were hunter-gatherers. I'm no anthropologist, but it seems to me that men are usually the hunters, and women gathered seeds and roots and prepared the food. If you talk to many women, a lot of them really hate hunting, but men generally don't, even the guys who don't hunt. Men seem to find something of a challenge in it—man versus nature and the idea of bringing home the winter's meat.

But there was once another kind of hunter, the one who eliminated danger to the tribe, and this type of hunter was probably the most revered because they had a lot of courage and made life safer for the others. This was the kind of guy who hunted grizzly bears and big predators.

OK, so much for my armchair anthropology. But I want to explain to you why a grown man who appeared to be sane in all other ways would voluntarily hunt grizzly bears. In retrospect, I think I was trying to prove my worth, as well as being an adrenaline junkie, and it almost cost me my life. Almost.

The real irony in this story is that when I got mauled, I wasn't even bear hunting—I was trying to get a deer to feed us through the winter. I had a tag for a mule deer, not a bear.

OK, it was autumn, and there I was, quietly tramping around in the thick forest, looking for deer. The Bella

Coola Valley is lush coastal rainforest and gets lots of rain, so deer hunting here is very different from that in drier places, much more difficult. You're always fighting your way through thick vegetation, and usually, you can't see far ahead. You can literally step on a sleeping grizzly before you see him.

Before I continue, let me say that getting mauled by a bear is a common theme around here, not just with the locals but with those who come in to trophy hunt. So, hunting in general around here can be a dangerous proposition.

On top of the thick vegetation, the valley goes straight up into steep mountains, so you'd better be in good shape to hunt here. And you can't avoid the mountains, as it's illegal to hunt within 400 meters of the highway, which goes right down the middle of the valley, for the most part. And a lot of this country isn't even hunt-able because of the thick vegetation.

I know people from the flatlands who feel claustrophobic in these rugged mountains, as they feel like the mountains are hugging them and they can't get away. If you like long vistas and wide open spaces, you'll still want to come visit, but you won't want to stay.

Back to the hunt. I knew of one wide drainage coming down off the mountains that had very thick vegetation but had lots of small open feed pockets, and I knew this would be where I would get my deer. I'd hunted it before and always been lucky there.

It was a steep climb at the bottom, but gradually leveled out enough that it could be hunted without killing yourself trying to climb and push through thick shrubs and ferns at the same time.

So, I'd been up there since early morning, walking an animal trail I'd found, stepping off it and hiding and waiting, then moving on. I hadn't seen hide nor hair of any deer so far, and it was now early afternoon.

What I had seen, though, was sign of bear—plenty of scat, and some of it was fresh. It was odd, as it's not unusual to come across bear scat, but there was too much, like a bear was frequenting the area, and I was beginning to think something was up. That, plus the total lack of any sign of deer, and I was beginning to feel a little leery.

After eating my lunch, I was actually considering leaving and going home for the day. I knew of a couple other places that might be good hunting, but I admit I was attached to this place, given my past successes there.

My enthusiasm was seriously waning, but I decided to give it another hour or two before giving up. I wondered if I weren't maybe being too noisy, as I'd left the animal trail and was pushing my way through a thick stand of alders, brushing against them as I passed.

Well, I suddenly froze, my instincts kicking in. I immediately knew I was in some kind of serious danger, but I didn't know from what. Somehow, my sixth sense had told me this, but it hadn't provided me with where it got the information. I'm a big believer in the sixth sense, and I think everyone has it. It's developed by using it, by being in places that are a little edgy.

I was in danger, I knew that. I slowly lifted my rifle, taking off the safety, and was ready to use it, when BAM! I was attacked from the rear by something that knocked me for a loop. I wasn't ready for the blow, and it knocked my rifle into the bushes and me in there behind it.

I quickly pulled myself into a fetal position. I was carrying bear spray in a holster that went around my torso, but I'd had the wind knocked out of me and wasn't thinking to reach for it. Before I could even look up to see what was after me, it had attacked again, this time making a huffing sound, so I knew it was a bear.

I felt a huge jaw grab my head, and I recall wondering if I'd somehow come between a sow and her cubs. Bears don't normally attack humans with no warning.

The bear bit me in the face and neck, and all I could think was, "OK, so this is how I'm going to die." I could feel the enormous weight of the animal as it partially stood on top of me. Time stopped, and it seemed like the mauling took forever, but I know it had to last only a few minutes.

The bear now grabbed my arm and began shaking it until I thought it would soon be ripped off. It all seemed painless, and I know now that I was in shock and my brain was blocking the trauma.

I now smelled what I took to be the smell of death—the smell of carrion. My mind was playing tricks on me, or so I thought. But it soon occurred to me, even as I was being mauled, that I'd stumbled upon the bear's cache. It had killed something, probably a deer, and buried it, returning to eat on the carcass.

Stumbling upon a bear cache is the only thing that's as dangerous as coming upon a sow and her cubs, and I'd managed to do exactly that. I now realized that I had to play dead if I wanted to have any chance at all. I had to convince the bear I was no threat to his food.

I went limp, the bear still chewing on my arm. It was probably the most difficult thing I'd ever done, to lie still while that bear was chomping on me, but I did. I figured I'd be dead soon enough anyway, so I might as well not prolong things.

I was feeling really lightheaded, and I knew I was beginning to lose a lot of blood, so I truly thought I was hallucinating when I heard a scream that made my ears almost vibrate, it was so loud. It echoed through the forest and seemed to go on and on and on.

Suddenly, the bear let go of my arm. I could see it stand up on its back legs and look around, as if trying to peer into the thick vegetation. It again began making that low huffing sound it had made while initially attacking me.

It now sounded like someone was tearing down the forest, trees breaking and falling into other trees, and this was accompanied by a loud stomping that made the ground beneath me literally shake. The bear turned, dropped onto all fours, and ran, quickly disappearing into the thick scrub.

I was amazed that I was still awake and hadn't passed out. As the noise came closer and closer, I had no idea what it was, but I became clear-headed enough to remember I had an emergency locater beacon, a PLB, in my back pocket.

I first tried to reach for it with my right hand, and almost passed out, as this was the arm the bear had mangled (60 stitches worth, to be exact). I swooned a little and almost passed out, then reached for it with my other arm, pulled it out, and activated it.

I really didn't think I had any chance at living through this, as I knew I was losing a lot of blood, but my stars were lucky that day, as things were lined up in a rare configuration that saved my life. The communication satellite happened to be right overhead and there was a military chopper in Bella Coola that day, for some reason or other.

Unbeknownst to me, within minutes of the PLB activation, my rescuers were on their way, having my GPS coordinates. Also on its way to me, however, was some force that left me mystified, something stomping through and tearing up the forest. It sounded furious.

I had no idea what it was, but I was grateful the bear had been afraid enough to leave me alone. In fact, it must have been really scared to leave its food cache. This fact gradually dawned on me—a bear is at the top of the food chain. What in the world would make it terrified enough to run off and leave its food? Obviously not humans, as it had already tried to kill one of those—me.

When I was a teenager, I'd discovered the works of Clayton Mack, a Nuxalk (Bella Coola) native hunter who led the wealthy on trophy bear hunts. I'd read his writings with great interest when I was a kid, as I was imagining myself to also be a great hunter in the making.

Most of his writings were about hunting grizzlies, but as I lay there, listening to this disturbing noise coming straight towards me, I suddenly flashed on a brief chapter he'd written about seeing a Sasquatch, or a Boq or Bukwa, as he said the natives called it. I'd read it with great interest, then later come to believe he was just pulling his readers' legs, having some fun, which he was known to do. Sasquatch was just a myth.

It seems amazing to me now, all this time later and knowing now that my arm was almost ripped off, that I had the presence of mind to even think about what was coming towards me, making all that noise.

But maybe, instead of a Sasquatch, it was another bigger bear, a bear the first knew and was afraid of. After all, bears knew each other and know who to steer clear of. Some bears will kill and eat their own species.

Somehow, though, I thought this had to be a Sasquatch, probably because a bear didn't scream like that. And it seemed now like maybe Clayton Mack wasn't kidding after all.

I was about to pass out when the noise finally stopped. Whatever it was, it had either calmed down or had realized a human was nearby. Was that why it was so angry, because I was there? Great, I thought, something new to worry about. But I really wasn't very worried, as I knew I was about to die regardless of who or what was there to hasten it along.

I'd had my eyes closed this whole time, trying not to pass out, but when I heard a low whistle right above me, I opened them.

There stood a most magnificent creature. I've read lots of Sasquatch and Bigfoot accounts since I recovered from all this, and almost everyone talks about how ugly they are, but to me, this giant creature standing above me was just magnificent.

He had slick black hair, and his eyes were the most incredible green color, like pools of that silty green glacial water you see in places like Emerald Lake at Yoho National Park. And every part of his huge body was in perfect shape, all rippled like a gold-medal Olympian, and you could tell he was the master of the mountains and forest, a fact that bear must've realized when it fled.

I was too near death to be afraid. What could he do to me? I was already dying.

He looked incredibly sad, then slowly reached down to touch my curly blonde hair—of which I had lots at the time, though now I'm going bald. He seemed fascinated by it.

Just then, I could hear the sound of a helicopter, and it was soon hovering overhead. My PLB! It had worked! I'd forgotten all about it. The Sasquatch also heard it and was long gone before the chopper even got near me.

The rest of the story you can guess. I was taken to the hospital in Williams Lake, where I nearly died from loss of blood, which they soon fixed with a transfusion. My arm required many stitches to fix up, and I have some major nerve damage, but I can make do with it and still drive and do basic things. I've learned to tie flies with my left hand, having given up hunting for fly-fishing.

And though everyone still calls me "Griz," it would be more appropriate to call me something like "Squatch," but I doubt if anyone would believe me if I told them the story.

But that's OK, as I feel kind of like I've been witness to something very special, and that's more than good enough.

12. Squatchin' at Sasquatch Provincial Park

I really got a kick out of this story. I heard it over a campfire near the Yellowstone River in Montana, and what I enjoyed most was the storyteller's honesty—he was determined to be a brave Bigfooter, but it seems he was human after all, just like the rest of us. And I bet you can guess where my next destination will be (along with Bella Coola), just as soon as I can get away.

—Rusty

Rusty, I've read all your books, as far as I know, and it seems there's one central theme to them—people have an encounter with a Bigfoot and are traumatized and generally swear to never camp or go outdoors again.

I know there are a few stories you've recounted where Bigfoot is helpful instead of terrifying (I'm thinking especially about the one with the girl in the wheelchair who's inspired by seeing a Bigfoot to get out and live her life), but in general, most folks seem to find what you call "the Big Guy" totally terrifying.

Well, I've thought about this a lot, and to me, this level of terror, where you get goosebumps and have the hair on your neck stand up, well, that almost speaks to me of something supernatural. People usually don't talk about grizzly bears or things that way—even though such predators can kill you.

OK, so where's this leading? Well, I've been what some might call a hard-core Bigfoot researcher for a number of years. I enjoy your stories, but I always thought the people in them were just a little on the soft side, even though some of them were seasoned outdoorsmen and seemed to have seen it all. I just always felt that they'd maybe let their prejudices run away with them upon seeing something they couldn't put in a box, something that society says doesn't exist, and they were just being downright superstitious.

So, I decided to really ramp up my game and do some serious Bigfooting. Sure, I'd been out lots of times camping and wood-knocking and doing everything I could think of to attract a Bigfoot, but I had yet to see or hear anything unusual. I really wanted to know if I would feel this way if I saw one—kind of like a coward, was how I felt about it.

I've always thought that Bigfoot was a real animal, but yet I wondered if it wasn't actually something from another realm, something out of our ordinary world of flesh and bone. This theory would explain a lot of things, like why there's never really been any bones found or definitive photographs taken. I'm still not sure about this, and there are still lots of things to explain.

It did worry me how I would react if I had an encounter and found Bigfoot to be something supernatural. But I figured if that were the case, at least I'd know and leave it alone, as I have no tolerance for things like that. My brain just can't deal with them.

So, how to find myself a Bigfoot? Lots of people have pondered this, all the other serious Bigfoot researchers, and I knew I wasn't unique in that regard, nor did I have anything new to offer on the subject.

I've thought about this over and over, and I finally decided that, if I wanted to increase my chances, I had to get to places where Bigfoot had been seen, and not by just one person, but by a number—what you call "Bigfoot Hotspots" in one of your books, Rusty.

I live in Carson City, Nevada, and there have been Bigfoot sightings near here, but I'd sure never had any luck, even up in the eastern Sierras. I'd also been Bigfooting in the Pacific Northwest, and I'm very aware of the miles and miles of thick timber there, but it just seemed to me that everybody and their dog went up there to do serious looking. Considering how many people already lived in the region, even if mostly in cities, I decided I wanted to go someplace more remote.

Well, I'd been in Canada when I was a teenager, going to Banff National Park with my parents, and I remembered it seeming like a wild place to me then. That was some 40 years ago, though, and I wondered if it hadn't been invaded by people, just like everyplace else.

The more I thought about it, the more logical it seemed that, if I was a serious Bigfooter, I needed to go into the remote reaches of Canada. I was thinking about places like the Yukon and Northwest Territories, which are way less populated.

My quandary was this—I had to work and didn't get enough time off to really get that far away, especially for long. I would spend most of my vacation time just getting there. I needed to find places a little closer to home.

So, I got out my map and started studying far western Canada, which would be a lot closer, a place I could maybe even drive to and spend time in the woods, even with my meager two-week vacation.

The first thing I thought of was the small town of Harrison Hot Springs in British Columbia. It was in the Fraser River Valley, which had been a Bigfoot Hotspot for many years, according to people like John Green, the Canadian Bigfoot researcher—or maybe I should call him a Sasquatch researcher, since that's what they call Bigfoot in Canada.

I got on the internet and found it on a map. It was almost due north of me, so I could just head straight up there, which made it seem closer. Of course, it wasn't that simple, but it seemed so at the time.

I really got a kick out of the Harrison Hot Springs webpage, which read, "All of the Village residents have a shared pet. He is a Sasquatch. No, he is not a collective hallucination. Look at it this way...if our water can sustain 10–14 foot sturgeon that we don't often see, and our mountains can sustain bear, deer and cougar even though we almost never see them, why can't our forests sustain a large hairy person? Just because you can't see him, doesn't mean we can't. (Mushrooms anyone?)"

Well, OK, so did they believe or didn't they? Like lots of people, including those who have actually had an encounter, they seemed wary of what people would think of them (it was the "mushrooms anyone" comment that made me believe this). I understood why, but I was determined to be straightforward and honest about any encounter I might have. In retrospect, maybe I was being a little self-righteous about the whole thing—I don't know.

I read as much as I could about encounters in that area, really burning up my internet usage, and there were actually quite a few, but nothing unusual. The encounters seemed pretty much like those I'd read about in the Pacific Northwest and other Bigfoot Hotspots, but there sure seemed to be a lot of them. Harrison Hot Springs was definitely a Sasquatch hangout.

It was then that I discovered Sasquatch Provincial Park, just north of Harrison Hot Springs. I was astounded at the park's name. The Canadians really must believe in Sasquatch—or else someone had a good sense of humor.

The park had three lakes in it—Hicks, Deer, and Trout—and was "renamed Sasquatch Park after the legendary Bigfoot, who is alleged to have roamed the area," or so read the webpage, which then added, "The park is characterized by a series of pocket lakes, a unique second-growth and birch forest, and scenic mountain ridges."

I studied the map, which showed Sasquatch Provincial Park being about two hours from Vancouver, making me wonder how many people frequented the area. I wanted a place really remote, and yet, I had to be realistic about my ability and time to get to such a place.

I decided I'd go up to the park and see what I could see. I'd just read about an encounter there, so maybe the Bigfoot were still there and the squatchin' would be good.

Harrison Hot Springs sits right smack in the middle of the Coastal Mountains next to Harrison Lake, pretty much surrounded by wilderness. Interestingly enough, the name Sasquatch is supposedly from the Coastal Salish "Sesquac," and means "a wild creature that's better left alone." I learned this from a guy I met in Harrison who was into the legends there and could recite every Sasquatch story in the area. I think he worked at the local tourism office, but I'm not sure. Anyway, him telling me that bit of trivia didn't help my disposition any, I can tell you that.

I was later told by another guy that the name Sasquatch came from the Chehalis people (now called the Sts'ailes), who once lived right there at Harrison. It was supposedly taken from their word "Saskehehavis," or "Sa:sq'ets," which means, "hairy man who can appear and reappear at will."

Anyway, by the time I got there (mid-July), it was raining and forecast to rain the whole week and a half that I was free to go squatchin'. I wasn't real happy about the weather, and hearing what the name Sasquatch meant— something one should stay away from, or hairy man who can appear at will—well, it didn't make me very eager to get out in the backcountry.

The encounter I'd read about had taken place in Sasquatch Provincial Park, so I headed up there through the rain, to Lakeside Campground, which was next to one of the lakes in the park, Deer Lake. The encounter had taken place in Site #12, so I was hoping that particular spot would be open, which it was. It was back a little away from the lake, so I was hoping the mosquitoes wouldn't be too bad (which they weren't, but only because it rained the entire time).

At least I had my pickup camper, which made camping in pouring rain a little more bearable, though not much. I backed into the spot, maybe subconsciously wanting to make sure I could get out fast if I needed to. So much for being brave, huh?

The campground was very green, surrounded by a thick forest with lush ferns and lots of little rivulets that I suspected only ran when it rained. And even though the encounter I'd read about had taken place over 10 years before, I was still hoping to see or hear a Sasquatch. It seemed like the perfect place.

I slept well that night, tired from all the driving, plus the light rain made a nice soft "white noise" on my roof. It also seemed unlikely that anything would be out in it, so I was pretty sure there wouldn't be any Sasquatch activity.

I was awakened by, so I thought, the need to take a bathroom break. As I opened my camper door and stepped outside, I heard something I can hardly describe—a long hair-raising howl from across the lake, followed by what sounded like a pack of coyotes going nuts, barking and yipping.

I did my business and quickly stepped back inside, locking the door and making sure the curtains were tightly closed. I'd gotten somewhat wet from the rain, so I dried myself off and crawled back into my sleeping bag, feeling chilled, even though it really wasn't cold.

Had I heard the mythical Sasquatch? I was awake enough to realize my chill wasn't from the rain or cool night, but was from my own fear. So much for being pragmatic and fearless. I felt a little humble that night.

I lay there, wishing I'd brought a recorder. That howl alone would've been worth way more than a recorder would have cost. I could then analyze it the next morning and see if it still sounded as creepy in the daylight as it did in the dark.

I finally drifted off, waking the next morning to yet more rain. What had been more of a mist was now an outright drizzle. I had a strange feeling, but couldn't quite put my finger on what it was or why.

But as I was drinking a hot cup of tea—how I always start my day—I suddenly remembered the weird howl. How could I forget something like that, even for a brief time? It was so strange, so weird.

I sat there, thinking, trying to recall exactly how it had sounded, when I suddenly decided it had to have been a wolf. After all, I was in British Columbia, and there were lots of wolves in this wild country, I was sure.

The more I thought about it, the more I was sure my Bigfooting was going to be a bust. How could I find anything in this rain?

I decided to hike around to the other side of the little lake and see if I could find any tracks, so I put on my Goretex jacket and pulled the hood close around my face. My hiking boots were waterproof (supposedly, though they ended up leaking). By now, it was raining pretty hard.

Deer Lake really isn't that big, and there's a road that goes on past it and on up to private land, so I walked down that and was soon on the other side of the lake. I then walked along the shoreline, looking for tracks, but found nothing and soon gave up.

By then, I was worried about getting disoriented in the rain, as it was hard to see anything. I knew I could follow the shoreline back to camp, but I now felt like I wanted to immediately get back. I was feeling nervous, and for no real reason, other than having heard a wolf the night before.

I kind of chided myself, once again recalling how I'd told myself I wouldn't be afraid around Bigfoot like everyone else was. Man, what hubris!

I finally made it back to my camper, where I fixed myself a cold sandwich and some more hot tea. The rain was really coming down now, and I wondered if the campground might start flooding. There were already big pools of water everywhere.

I decided I should batten down the hatches and be ready to pull out just in case, so I put everything away that I wasn't using. All I would have to do if I needed to leave at that point was put a couple of small things away and drive off.

The afternoon wore on, and the few times I stuck my head outside to scope things out, I noticed more and more campers had left. The campground had been about half full when I arrived, but now it seemed like I was the only one there. I'd read that the pocket lakes in Sasquatch Provincial Park were popular for boating and fishing, but there was no one out on Deer Lake, and I suspected the other lakes were the same.

That made me feel even more uncertain, like maybe I should head back to Harrison Hot Springs and stay there. I could park in an empty lot or something.

Oh, I forgot to tell you something. On my way back from the other shore, I had found something of interest—a broken tree. It was a small alder, maybe about four inches across, and it had been neatly broken in two. The break looked fresh, as the wood was still nice and white, and it had been broken at a height I couldn't begin to reach, maybe about eight feet up.

I puzzled over this, wondering what had happened. There had been no wind, and nothing else was damaged, none of the shrubs around the tree. It simply looked like someone had reached up and broken the top of the tree off, and the broken part was nowhere to be found. It just seemed really odd and made me increase the speed of my pace.

After sitting in my camper for hours, reading a book and eating way too many Little Debbie Snackcakes, which I'd brought from home, I decided to try it again and go for a walk. This time, I would just walk around the campground. I'd lost any interest in exploring the lake or anyplace else, especially with nobody around.

I'd been right—there wasn't another soul in the campground. It appeared that the majority of people have more brains than I do and had gone home. I again thought about leaving and going to Harrison. Heck, maybe it was time to go on home myself. I could spend the rest of my vacation where it was dry and the sun was shining.

I'd driven a long ways to go squatchin', and now it looked like a total bust. But I'm stubborn, so I decided to give it another day or two. I'm not much of one for restaurants or shopping, or I might have been happy hanging around Harrison Hot Springs.

I'd come to find Bigfoot, and with everyone else gone, it dawned on me that maybe my chances were now better. If Sasquatch really were as shy as people said, they might be more inclined to come into the campground with everyone gone. Maybe they'd come in to see if anyone had left any food.

I was now back to my truck when I saw something that left me feeling very strange—the top of that little alder tree was right there on my picnic table. That really freaked me out, I can say, and I'm not sure why I didn't just get in my truck and leave right then and there, but I didn't. I think I was truly beginning to want my trip to amount to something more than sitting in the rain and was reluctant to admit it was a bust.

But the tree had been clear around on the other shore of the lake, so someone had to have carried the top all the way back here to my camp. It was long and awkward to carry, and besides, why would anyone want to do that?

But what really gave me pause was realizing that whoever had left it did so while I'd been out walking around the park. There was no one else here! I looked around for tracks, but there was nothing—the gravel wouldn't have shown anything anyway. I thought about walking back up to the road and seeing if I could track back to the little tree, but I admit I was now too nervous to even want to be outside.

I climbed into the cab of my truck and sat there, the rain still coming down, making little miniature streams across my windshield. I knew I should leave, but something held me back.

I think it was pride. I didn't want to admit to myself that something that inconsequential would make me abort a serious trip like this. I was already having problems coming to grips with how scared I'd been about the howl. My self-image was taking a beating, and I needed to regain my confidence. I decided to stay.

Later, I decided that the tree thing really hadn't been inconsequential, and I'd seriously misjudged the event. Having someone carry a broken tree back into your camp means they had to have followed you, and having someone do that is actually pretty unsettling, especially in an empty campground in Canada.

I got out, locked the cab, then went back into my camper. I would just hang out and read a book, then go to bed early. I decided I would leave the next day. At least that was the plan, anyway. No point sitting for a week in a camper in the rain. My Bigfoot hunting expedition would just have to go down in history as a big bust, unless I counted the tree as being related to Bigfoot activity.

The rest of the day was pretty boring, for sure. I'm an active person and actually don't read much, so sitting in a small camper listening to it rain isn't my idea of fun. I did get out a couple of times and walk around some, but not far, and I finally gave up and got into my sweats and crawled into bed, even though it was still daylight outside.

When you have nothing to do, it's easy to drift off into sleepyland, as you have no mental stimulation. I went to sleep, not realizing the lack of stimulation was about to change.

It was about midnight when I woke. I'd had a beer before going to bed, and I knew it would have its effect on me in the middle of the night, but so be it. I opened the camper door and was suddenly afraid to go out into the dark. I noticed the rain had let up, and I could even see a couple of stars overhead.

I finally persuaded myself to step down and go pee in a nearby bush. But just as I was getting back into the camper, suddenly feeling a sense of panic, something smashed against the rear bumper, almost hitting me.

I jumped inside and locked the door. What the heck! I stood there, listening, but all was still. I finally opened the door a crack and shined my flashlight out to see what had hit the truck. I'll be darned if it wasn't that very same tree top.

I sat down, now shaking. Someone or something was out there. I felt totally defenseless, and I knew I needed to run to the cab and drive away, but I was too scared to even move.

Oy vey, as one of my friends would say (or something like that). I was suddenly paralyzed. What could I do? I felt as if my life was at stake, but as I sat there and nothing else happened, I was able to gradually relax a little.

It was the middle of the night, and someone had thrown the tree at me and missed, and I suspected that "someone" was exactly why I was here, to have a long-awaited Bigfoot encounter. I'd been looking for Bigfoot for years, and now that it appeared to be around, I was going to run off like a scared rabbit.

I thought about how I had ridiculed the people in the stories I'd read who had been scared of Bigfoot. My sense of superiority was now gone, but I was again determined to try to stay as long as I could. I wanted nothing more than to know that Bigfoot really existed. Some people would say that I already had enough evidence, but I wanted to actually see one. It had become a lifelong quest.

I managed to talk myself into being calm and climbed back into bed.

It was then that I could hear someone talking. I strained to hear, but it sounded like several big guys murmuring, and by that, I mean they were talking in low voices and I couldn't decipher the words.

This went on for some time, and it sounded like there was several of whatever they were, over in the trees behind the campsite across from me. I quietly opened the window by my head just a crack so I could hear better.

Now I could make out the sound more clearly, but I was still unable to decipher any words. It sounded like people with lisps would talk, a lot of "s" sounds. The voices were very very low, like a large creature might have.

I was no longer scared, but felt a heightened sense, a rush of adrenaline. Was I listening to several Bigfoot talking? How many people got to hear something like this?

Well, all of a sudden I was scared again—actually, terrified. Something big had slammed against the side of my camper, not all that far from my head. I sat up and kicked off my sleeping bag, slipping into my hiking boots, wanting to be ready in case I needed to try and make a break. My pickup has a sliding back window that leads into the camper, but I'm a big guy, and there was no way I could get through there. I would have to make a run for the cab, hoping nothing hit me.

As I sat there, contemplating what could be an early death, I heard the voices again, but now they were louder. And even though they were now clear, I couldn't understand a word that was being said, though it did sound very much like a language.

Something again hit the truck, and now one of the voices was talking excitedly, much louder. A second voice seemed to answer back, and before long, it sounded exactly like they were arguing. A third voice sounded out from the background, not as loud and a little higher-pitched. I wondered if it weren't a female.

It seemed like I was listening to a Bigfoot argument, right there outside my trailer. Were they arguing about me? Oh man, now I was beyond terrified. What if they decided to kill me? Sure, Bigfoot was supposedly a gentle giant, but these voices didn't sound so gentle.

Suddenly, something again struck the side of my camper, something big. I jumped to my feet. I started to yell out, but thought better of it. I just needed to get out of there, jump into the cab and flee. But I was too scared.

The voices were now very loud, and one sounded for the life of me like it was yelling. A second voice yelled back, and then I heard a sound like a big branch hitting my picnic table.

That was it. I had to get out of there. Now, for some reason, I felt totally unafraid. I carefully grabbed my keys, making sure I had the starter key right in my hand, then I pushed the unlock button, unlocking the cab electronically from inside the camper.

I paused, listening. Did these creatures (who I now knew had to be Canadian Sasquatch) recognize the sound of a car being unlocked? If they hung out around people much, they had to. Were they now waiting for me to get out of the truck, knowing people unlock their vehicles right before they get into them?

I felt like I'd screwed up, so I relocked it. Surely, if they knew what it all meant, they would no longer be expecting me to get out. I was now scared again.

Boom! Another branch or something hit the side of the camper. I was now getting really concerned about the damage they had to be doing.

Then I got mad. I'd worked hard for that camper. It was my freedom camper, the only way I had to get away from everything when I got stressed, which was often. I was a machinist, and it could be hard work. And for these creatures to be destroying my rig for no reason, well, that just irritated the heck out of me.

I jumped from the back of the camper, not even really thinking about what I was doing, unlocked the cab, and jumped in. The adrenaline was now pumping, as I started the truck and put it into first gear, turning on the lights.

I pulled out, and as I turned onto the campground road, my lights shone on three huge creatures standing near the edge of the trees. One held a branch as if ready to throw it, but when my lights hit them, they all turned and ran.

I realized on one level that I'd finally seen the object of many many hours of searching—trips into the wilderness, uncomfortable nights calling into the woods like a fool, whacking on trees—three Bigfoot had been standing right there, but it all seemed unreal.

I drove like a madman, and it seemed to take forever to get out of the park and back to the main highway. Once I reached Harrison Hot Springs, I stopped and parked along a back street. It was then that I realized I was shaking.

I got out of the cab and climbed into the camper, hoping to get some sleep, but suddenly felt claustrophobic. I climbed back into the cab and slept there for what was left of the night.

The next day, I checked out the damage to my camper, and it really wasn't too bad, just a few dents that I hoped I could pound out when I got home.

I was all ready to head out, yet I didn't want to go, as I still had the majority of my vacation left. I only got two weeks a year, and I decided I wanted to stay, but not in the woods in my camper.

I walked around Harrison Hot Springs for awhile, and finally I went into a small lodge to see if they had a room. They were booked full, probably because of all the rain. I wondered if I would be able to find anything at all.

I got to talking to a fellow there, a guest, and one thing led to another, and he told me about this big event the town has called Sasquatch Days, held each June. Apparently the Sasquatch is the symbol of the native people there, the Sts'ailes First Nation, and they hold it as sacred. (I didn't mention my encounter, nor did I tell him that I didn't find anything very sacred about having my camper damaged.)

To make a long story short, he told me about this nice B&B that might have rooms, as they were in an out of the way place, on over near Agassiz on the other side of Harrison Lake. I called, and sure enough, they had a room.

Funny enough, it was called the Sasquatch Crossing Eco Lodge and was run by the native people. I stayed there the rest of my vacation, over a week, and I can tell you, we had some really good talks about Sasquatch.

I finally even told the hosts about my encounter, and they seemed to regard me differently after that, like I was someone special. I had a super nice time there, and it even stopped raining. I could finally see the gorgeous mountains that surround the Fraser Valley.

Anyway, I didn't mean to make this into such a long story, but after I got home and had some time to analyze the whole thing, I realized I wasn't nearly as brave and macho as I thought I was.

So, Rusty, you can put my story right in there with the others—brave man has Bigfoot encounter and nearly pees his pants. But I *will* go camping again—maybe, anyway.

About the Author

Rusty Wilson is a fly-fishing guide based in Colorado and Montana. He's well-known for his dutch-oven cookouts and campfires, where he's heard some pretty wild stories about the creatures in the woods, especially Bigfoot.

Whether you're a Bigfoot believer or not, we hope you enjoyed this book, and we know you'll enjoy Rusty's many others, the first of which is *Rusty Wilson's Bigfoot Campfire Stories*. Rusty's books come in ebook format, as well as in print and audio.

You'll also enjoy Rusty's unique book, *Wild and Weird Campfire Stories*, featuring the award-winning *Ghost of the Canadian Mountie*.

Suspend disbelief and go on a road trip with a Bigfoot in Rusty's book, *The Bigfoot Runes*, an adventure like none you'll ever read again. One reviewer says: *One of the best books I have ever read. I love and have read all of Rusty Wilson's Bigfoot stories, but this one was just amazing.*

And don't forget Rusty's *Chasing After Bigfoot*, an adventure that will have you on the edge of your seat.

Also, you'll enjoy *The Ghost Rock Cafe* by Chinle Miller, a Bigfoot mystery.

We'd also like to mention a book by Brad Morris, *Stalked! My Encounter with a Colorado Bigfoot*, a wild story of dread and horror in the remotest part of Colorado. Brad Morris relates this terrifying tale of an encounter with a Bigfoot at 14,000 feet in the Colorado Rockies, where he finds something that will change his life forever.

One reviewer says: *Morris tells a great story of nature's fury, but also its benevolence. Whether you believe or not, this a great adventure tale.*

Check us out at yellowcatbooks.com and thanks for reading!

Made in the USA
Middletown, DE
03 September 2021

47525909R00099